GRINDHOUSE PURGATORY
VOL. 1, ISSUE 15

EULOGY: SID HAIG 1939-2019	2
"YOU HERE TO TALK OR DRINK? WE'RE DOIN' BOTH."	4
SID HAIG - ONE ON ONE	7
A BRIEF ELEGY FOR MOVIE STAR SID HAIG	32
SPIDER BABY, OR THE MADDEST STORY EVER TOLD (1967)	34
BLACK MAMA WHITE MAMA (1973) & *SAVAGE SISTERS* (1974)	41
SAVAGE SISTERS: SID GOES PSYCHO	44
THE HOST: HAIG & HILL, TOGETHER FOR THE FIRST TIME	46
"I LIVE, AND I DIE, BY THE CRYSTALS!"	49
SID, PAM AND JACK: FUN IN THE PHILIPPINES	52
SID HAIG: IMPOSSIBLE MISSIONS HEAVY	54
SID HAIG IN *BUSTING* (1974)	56
THE BLU-RAY REPORT: *BEYOND ATLANTIS*	58
SID BY THE SEA	61
WONDER WOMEN: SID'S FOURTH FILIPINO FILM	63
WHAT IT MEANS TO BE AN "ICON"	66
PIT STOP (1969) REVIEW	68
PIT STOP: JACK HILL AND SID HAIG'S WILD MASTERPIECE	70
SID AND JACK AND PAM	77
WOMAN HUNT: SID AT HIS SLEAZY BEST	81
CREATURE COMFORT	83

Front Cover: © Phillip R. Rogers. Back Cover: © Misty Wood.
Editor-in-Chief: Pete Chiarella. Editor: Mike Watt. Assistant Editor: Kimberlee Mathies

Contributors: Bill Adcock, Aaron AuBuchon, Dr. Rhonda Baughman, David Beckham, Ken Brunette, Terrence Cain, Mike Haushalter, Robert Morgan, David Phillips, John Rieber, Joe Ripple, Robert Segedy, John Shatzer, Ross Snyder, Douglas Waltz.

© 2020 Happy Cloud Media, LLC. - ISBN: 978-1-951036-17-1

Grindhouse Purgatory is published twice per year by Happy Cloud Media, LLC. All rights reserved. **The views and opinions expressed within this publication are not necessarily or usually those of the publisher.** No part of this publication can be duplicated in any way without express permission of the publisher. Except for the pictures. The pictures we already stole. Knock yourself out.

EULOGY: SID HAIG 1939-2019

It isn't often that you meet a true legend, but a lot of us did when Sid Haig started doing conventions. Sid was one of the real grindhouse icons, starting with *Spider Baby* in 1963 and ending with *Genuine Risk* in 1990. He gave up acting in 1992 as he said that he was tired of pointing a gun in people's faces. Oddly, that is the same reason Lee Van Cleef quit acting, but was brought back by Sergio Leone.

Quentin Tarantino contacted Sid and wanted him in *Jackie Brown*. Sid said that Tarantino wouldn't take no for an answer. So Sid was cast as a judge and star, Pam Grier, who had worked with Sid in the past, wasn't told he would be there. She almost spit out her teeth when she did that scene. Then Sid was sent a script from Rob Zombie for *House of 1000 Corpses*. Sid, as the clown Capt. Spaulding was an instant hit with new horror fans.

Now Sid was a horror star. But he never started out as one. The closest he came to horror was *Beyond Atlantis* (and maybe *Wonder Women*). He was primarily an action star. When *House* became a hit, a sequel, *The Devil's Rejects*, became a bigger hit with Sid. This would be Sid's second coming and even though Rob Zombie used him in *Lords of Salem*, his biggest booster, Tarantino never had any work for him after *Kill Bill 2*.

So Sid was cast in an endless bunch of low budget, grade-B horror films. Some good, others atrocious. But he was working, and doing a lot of horror conventions. I first met him when he first appeared at Chiller. We hit it off and were friends. Sid was made a lot of promises that weren't kept. But Sid loved his fans and never screwed them. While other stars charged fans to take a picture with their own camera, Sid wouldn't he also wouldn't ass-rape the fans with high prices at his table. I was his personal "security" at one convention and saw firsthand what a generous, humble guy he was.

But life gets in the way sometimes and we lost touch. Sid was at a lot of cons, but I wasn't. Perhaps due to my habit of calling out rip-off scumbag promoters and "managers," I'm not welcome in certain places, like I give a shit. So it was only until recently, that Sid contacted me. We were cordial and caught up. Only I didn't know how sick he was and that the cancer he beat came back. Then word came out that he had a fall and was hospitalized.

We all thought that he would rally, which he did for a short while. Then I got a call that he passed and was asked to keep it to myself, which I did. I posted his passing when I got permission to. Everyone was devastated, it was like a family member passed, and Sid was family to a lot of us. I don't know of any fan that met Sid and didn't walk away with a smile on their face. It was the end of an era as Sid was one of the guys who put the grind in grindhouse.

Speaking for myself, it was an honor and a privilege to know him and call him a friend. I cried when I got the news, and I'm not ashamed to admit it. Thank you, Sid, for all you have done in your close to six decades as an actor. I learned a lot hanging with you and when you left, the world lost a very decent and caring human being. I hope what we have done here in this magazine, is a fitting tribute to your memory. RIP, my friend, you will live on through your work and you will never be forgotten.

Tutti Fuckin Fruity,
XXX, 42P

Sid and Suzy.
(Copyright unknown, all rights reserved)

"YOU HERE TO TALK OR DRINK? WE'RE DOIN' BOTH."
By Mike Watt

Suzy, Amy Lynn Best, and Sid.
(Photo copyright Happy Cloud Media, LLC)

Sid Haig was responsible for many of my favorite blackouts. So many of our convention stories—the good ones, the ones we can only tell in certain mixed company—begin with the sentence, "So, we were drinking up in Sid's room…"

For many of us doing the con circuits during the 2000s, drinking in Sid's room after hours was like drinking with royalty. If you were in that room, you were family.

At the time Sid Haig started doing conventions, he was in high demand due to his "return" role as the maniacal and hysterical Captain Spaulding in Rob Zombie's *House of 1,000 Corpses*. It is for this role, for writing the role for Sid, that many of us pay grudging thanks to Zombie. Because the role gave Haig's career another wind. When we found ourselves in Sid's room one night, I hadn't even seen *House,* even though it starred my friend Bill Moseley, who told me about the film's existence in the first place, during an interview for *Cinefantastique*. I just wanted to party with a guy who had worked with damned near everybody--Corman, Kubrick, Aldrich, the great Jack Hill, Pam Grier, Lee Marvin, Don Adams, Buck Henry--name someone, Sid knew them. And I wanted to hear those stories.

Unfortunately, it's impossible to pay attention to a story, no matter how hard you try, when you're graying out during the conversation. You didn't *have* to drink with Sid—you didn't *have* to do anything for or with Sid to enjoy his company--but that's generally what ended up happening.

Our entry into the suite of royalty came when shock author and friend Joe Knetter first invited us. I don't remember the show—either a Chiller or a Monster Mania—I just remember Sid entering with a gallon of Captain Morgan, taking a swig, topping it off with Coca Cola, then passing it around. I remember Amy Lynn Best, my wife and partner, agreeing to Sid's challenge to keep up with him, drink for drink.

Neither of us remember much after that.

Another show or two later, Sid himself swings by our table-"You guys joining us? We're up in Room 1020 (or whatever)." That invitation meant everything. A personal invite from a man whom I'd admired forever? Suddenly, we were *in*. We were *somebody* by royal decree. That night, a fan had made a hookah for Sid, out of what looked like a car muffler. I wasn't a big smoker then, but I'd be *damned* if I was going to pass up the opportunity to smoke hash (I think, hope?) with Sid Motherfuckin' Haig.

See, where the new kids only knew Sid from *House* and *The Devil's Rejects*, we knew him from syndicated TV. Turn on anything made between 1970 and 1990, Sid was in it. He was two separate heavies in *Get Smart*. He was a biker in a cell next to George Peppard's Hannibal in *The A-Team*. I barely remember *Mission: Impossible*, but I remember Sid being there. And, of course, as a kid from the '70s, I remember him as Dragos from the otherwise lousy *Jason of Star Command*. Forget the boring, clean-cut, pre-fab furniture hero that was Craig Littler's Jason. I loved the evil cyborg, with his red laser eye. Dragos was the only character who seemed *alive*. Jimmy Doohan certainly phoned it in-no Scotty here. (And even as a kid, I hated that little "Wiki" robot. I'd rooted for Dragos to destroy it like the lousy knock-off toy that it was.)

Sid was always doing things that made him stand out in the background. In Robert Aldrich's gleefully sadistic *Emperor of the North Pole*, Sid shows up in a hobo camp, a rooster under his arm. The rooster is partially explained, but your eye is constantly drawn to those crowd scenes, wanting to know more about the guy carrying around the live poultry. Even when Borgnine and Marvin start wailing on each other on top of the train, you wonder, "What happened to the dude with the chicken?" At least I did. In a sea of interesting faces, Sid's was the best.

If there's a modern definition of *mensch* in the horror community, it comes with Sid's picture. He could be grumpy, but I never saw him unkind. At one show, we hadn't seen him in over a year, and he looked exhausted. He was still smiling, still signing photos for anyone who wanted one, still giving shit to his neighbors who were selling their signatures for $50 or more when nothing on his table cost more than $20, but he didn't seem himself. Fans started bitching that he wasn't fellating them after time spent in line. Turns out, the man had walking pneumonia! We thought he "looked a little tired." That's a *mensch*, friends, any way you slice it.

One night we discovered one of my oldest friends, a non-industry guy, was getting married to his longtime girlfriend. Sid left an exaggeratedly drunken message of congratulations on his voicemail. When we returned, my buddy called me back. "Did...did you have something to do with Sid Haig calling me?"

"Like I could get Sid to do anything," I said. And it was true. Sid just grabbed our phone and did it for fun. Because he was a mensch.

Sid was kind to everyone so long as you didn't go out of your way to piss him off. Everyone was welcome but not *everyone* was welcome. He was choosy about who got to walk through that door.

My clearest memory: on a similar hard-drinkin' night, which appealed to the romantic journalist in me, after finishing a round of political banter with Michael Berryman, and a discussion of classic rock with Ari Lehman, I collapsed into a chair next to Sid's fiancee and soon-to-be wife (if memory and timelines serve), Susan Olberg, who we called "Suz". I nudged her foot with mine, nodded towards Sid.

"Hey, Suz, you hittin' that?"

She smiled, "You mean that fine piece of Armenian man over there?"

"Yeah."

"Oh, yeah."

Sid and Suz chose their family. When Bill Moseley came in barefoot and attacked a birthday cake with a butcher knife, he was family. Knetter and his never-empty cup, he was family. It didn't matter if you were in the business or not, if you were in that room, you were family.

For a while, we were lucky to be family. And now my family has shrunk a little and we're all a little worse off for our loss.

But we will always be better off for the time we got to spend with--and I use none of these words lightly--a fucking legend.

RIP, my friend, and thank you.

SID HAIG - ONE ON ONE

I had discovered Sid Haig during my Drive-In /Grindhouse days. *The Big Bird Cage, Savage Sisters, Busting Coffee*, and his frequent TV appearances during the '70s. Then he just vanished off the map. When I was involved with The Chiller Theatre Convention, I often brought up his name as a potential guest, but no one knew how to contact him. Then Sid resurfaced with a short appearance as a judge in *Jackie Brown*.

His big comeback role would be Captain Spaulding in *House of 1,000 Corpses*. Sid became the "new" horror star. He was booked into the Chiller Convention the same time I was involved in the documentary, *Unconventional*. Sid had a huge line all weekend and we struck up a friendship there. It was then I found out what a humble, charitable man Sid was. It was when that tsunami had hit parts of Asia and Sid was raising money at his table to help the victims. Chiller had an auction then, and I put some stuff in for the tsunami victims also. I handed Sid I think $90. I said it's for the cause.

Sid returned for the next show and we had more time to talk. I left Chiller when he appeared a third time. I was now at Monster Mania, but that would be short-lived. Sid was booked there. Myself and a couple of others usually booked a suite so we could party. We got in Thursday night before the show started. Sid was there too. There was a lame event put together, something like "Coffee & Cookies with the Stars."

It was embarrassing. A geek would announce each guest as they entered the room. Sid took one look and said to me "You guys have a suite? I'll meet you there." So we hung out with Sid and his wife, Suzi. We smoked weed and drank until half O'Clock in the morning. Sid told us stories of working in the Philippines with Pam Grier, Jack Hill, Vic Diaz, and others. Monster Mania became another case of the promoter becoming the star of his own show. I left and was

*Sheri Moon Zombie, Sid, Bill Moseley in **The Devil's Rejects**.*
(Copyright Lionsgate, All Rights Reserved)

done with conventions at that point. But Sid stayed in touch.

I started a podcast on Jackalope Radio with Todd Sheets. Sid was now having problems with Monster Mania. I think it was over money owed. I know there was a lot of shit going on. I invited Sid to be on the show to tell his side of things. He was livid and wanted to vent. Before the show, he called me. "Look, I took the booking because I didn't want to disappoint my fans." Sid was one guy who really appreciated his fans and always kept his prices low. When others were charging fans to take pictures with their own cameras, Sid didn't.

"I still want to do your show, but not talk about the Monster Mania situation." I agreed. When we did the show, it crashed. Not being a tech guy, it had something to do with bandwidth. We got so many hits that it crashed the system. Luckily, we taped it so we could fix the problem and air it again. At the end, proving that I was a better man, I put over his MM appearance.

Sid appeared on my show a couple of more times, then asked me for a favor. He was doing a con called Rock & Shock in Massachusetts. He had two stalkers. He wanted me as his "security" for the weekend as the promoters didn't take the threat seriously. I told him no problem until I found out one stalker was a woman. I don't hit chicks, so I brought an old friend of his wife's, Dana, with me.

I didn't think anything would happen, but the guy showed up Friday night. Sid was livid. The promoters tried to calm him down but he wasn't having it. I told him don't worry. You have to go to the crapper, I stand outside the door. You go eat, I stand and watch. He pretty much told the promoters that if the guy showed up Saturday, Sid would walk out. Thankfully he didn't.

Here I saw firsthand Sid's love for his fans. He was right next to Bill Moseley. I played photographer for any fan who wanted a picture taken with Sid.

The running gag for the weekend was when fans would ask if there would be a sequel to *The Devil's Rejects*. Sid would turn to Bill and say, "You know why there won't be a sequel?

"Why is that, Sid?" Bill would ask.

"Because we're both fuckin' dead!"

Around that time, I pitched an idea to Sid about doing a "shoot" interview. The "shoot" interview was created by RF Video, a DVD company that puts out wrestling DVDs. In wrestling language, a shoot is real and a work is fake. Wrestlers doing a shoot interview usually tell the truth about the business. So Sid was interested. I sent him some of the shoot DVDs I had so he could see what I was talking about.

He was down for it, we tried to do it at this con, but we were all too tired to make it work. Sid was booked at a new convention, Saturday Nightmares. It was to be held at The Sheraton Hotel in East Rutherford, NJ, former home of the Chiller Convention. The promoter

remembered me as the announcer from Chiller, so he hired me to announce his show. I also did a great interview with Sid. We wanted to focus on his entire career, not just the Rob Zombie films. So what do you think the first fan question was? "Are you doing a sequel to *The Devil's Rejects*?" We had stated early on that he wasn't, but it obviously didn't sink in.

We decided to do his interview after the con shut down. We went to the Tick Tock Diner on Route 3, a place Sid liked on his previous trips out here. Then we went back to his room where we did this interview for almost four hours. We had it edited and we sent Sid a copy for his approval. I had high hopes as this was the ultimate piece on his career. Then something happened. A miscue of sorts and we lost contact.

The miscue was that Shock Stock, a con in Canada, wanted Sid as a guest. They didn't have his contact information, so they asked me. I called Sid and told them what they wanted. I put them in touch, Sid had certain requirements to get there. Two things happened, his flights were really at a late hour and he was pulled aside by customs. He wasn't happy. And he was upset with me because I set it up. I didn't make a nickel on his appearance, I thought I was doing him a favor. But, as you'll read, this is a brutal business and friendships sometimes take a back seat. I ate the project, but losing a friend was worse than losing the time and money spent on it.

I did try to reach out, but Sid went with a manager who didn't treat him right. He was appearing at cons that I didn't frequent and always had a project going on. He wanted, I was told, to come back to Cinema Wasteland, but that didn't happen either.

This was almost ten years ago. I know Sid was having major health issues. He reached out to me on Facebook under his real name. We were cordial as I asked him how he was doing and hoped he was well. I found out he had beaten colon cancer, but it came back. Then he had an accident and we lost him. I, along with the rest of his fans, was devastated. I had enjoyed my relationship with him and considered him a friend. This is a fucked up business we are in. I had total respect for the man and he is a legend.

I knew I had a copy of what was meant to be a Sid Documentary. I know he had done a ton of interviews since this one, but we covered things that usually didn't come up in other interviews. I will transcribe this to the best of my ability as a tribute to Sid and his many fans.

***

Pete: Right now as we talk, you are celebrating 50 years as an actor.

Sid: Right, this is my 50th year in the business. I just turned 73 and I feel like I'm 25. Going to keep on going.

Pete: What got you into acting?

Sid: Well, I was an only child and had made up friends. Not only was I an only child, I was the only kid in a four block area. So I created my own world and actually, I didn't know it at the time, I was acting. It came naturally to me. So I signed up for dancing lessons and I really took to it. At the age of 7, I was getting paid to dance. Then I got into music, then acting, it sorta just evolved. It just took over my life. So here I am 50 years and still doing it.

Pete: Talking about the music, you actually had a band, The T-Birds, and you were the drummer.

Sid: I played with some bands, then friends put together a band, first called The Spades. We were picked up by a small label, Dice Records. We got airplay. Then Sam Cooke's label, Keene Records, offered us a contract. We took it, changed the band's name to The T-Birds and it just took off from there. The problem with that whole thing was that we were working our asses off and not seeing any money. I was practical then, even as a kid. This music thing isn't working, so I dropped it. I was acting though college and a friend suggested I go study acting at The Pasadena Playhouse. So I enrolled and it was pretty cool. A lot of great actors came out of there, Dustin Hoffman, Gene Hackman, etc. It was actor's boot camp for two years. We started at 7:30 am and didn't finish until after 11pm. Then go home and do homework, then be back at 7:30 am to do it all over again. This prepared you for working 16-18 hours straight as a professional actor.

Pete: What are your memories of *Spider Baby* and your character, Ralph?

Sid: Every five years that film gets a new group of fans. Ralph was the oldest of the Merryman family and the older he got, the more he regressed. So Ralph was almost there, he didn't speak, he grunted. So to prepare, I went to the zoo and watched how the primates behaved, interacted with each other, etc. Then I'd go to the playground and watched the kids and see how they interacted with each other. So I put the two together and that became Ralph. Jack Hill, the director, wanted me to come in and meet the producers. Remember, I didn't have any lines, so I went in, picked my nose, picked at my toes, started drooling. The producers were like, "What did we get ourselves into? This guy is a total looney." But it all worked out.

Working with Lon Chaney, Jr., was an amazing thing for me as I grew up watching his films. The first couple of day I was just in awe of him. So we are shooting and Jack asks me to go get Lon. So I go to his trailer and say Mr. Chaney jack is ready for you. He says to me, "Knock off the 'mister.' I'm Lon, you're Sid, and we are working together.' That's the kind of guy he was. Then I met Mantan Moreland, who I remembered from all the Charlie Chan movies. He was a great guy and fun to be around. He was just so happy to be working. After the Charlie Chan stuff ended, he sorta fell off the planet. He was thankful that people remembered him.

Pete: *Spider Baby* was on the Drive-In /Grindhouse circuit for over 30 years. Bunch of different titles, *The Maddest Story Ever told, The Liver Eaters*, and others. Then it was restored for its 30th anniversary.

Sid: That was amazing. Johnny Legend was instrumental in getting some lost footage together and cleaning some other stuff up. We had it play at the New Art theater in Hollywood. When I got there, there was a line around the block. I was freaked, I thought how do people even know about this? I expected maybe 50 people, not a sellout. There were people in their 40s, 50s, teenagers, it was amazing to me. Every five years we get a whole new audience as people keep rediscovering this film.

I did *Pit Stop* (1969) for Jack after that, another amazing experience. It was a grindhouse film about stock car racing, pure Guerrilla filmmaking. Not just stock car racing—figure-eight racing. Roger Corman gave Jack Hill $35K to make the film. We had over 100 cars and drivers. Now, you might ask, how did we get that? Well, I'll tell you. We got Ascot Park, by making the

Carol Ohmart, Sid, Beverly Washburn, Lon Chaney, Jr., in Jack Hill's **Spider Baby.**
(Copyright American General Pictures. All Rights Reserved)

owner of that race track the announcer for the races. We made the doctor of the clinic—where they took the injured racers—play the doctor in the film. The racers would hang out at the bar across the street, so we made the owner the bartender. George Barris, the custom car guy [who built the 1966 Batmobile for *The Batman* TV Show], we used his shop. Then we called a brewery and told them that we are making a movie with five party scenes in it. They said, "Where do you want the beer?" So we had a beer truck on set. So add all this together, and that's how we got the film done. There was a young woman in the film, Ellen McRae, who we now know as Ellen Burstyn. It was her first film.

Pete: Weren't you supposed to be in those Boris Karloff films that Jack hill shot?

Sid: Jack was offered four films starring Boris Karloff from a Mexican company. Jack called me and wanted me to costar with Karloff in all four films. I was like "Where do I show up?" It would have been amazing to do that. We were all set and ready to go, then Karloff's doctor said there is no way that he is going to Mexico, he won't come back alive. So they decide to shoot Boris's scenes in the States. Then I get a call from the Union [Screen Actors Guild] telling me that I may not do this film. I said, "Why?" They said because the Mexican film company is not signatory with the Union.

So I said, "Karloff is doing the film, right?" They say, "Yes, he is."

I say, "Stop me if I'm wrong, but his union card is exactly like mine." And this idiot at the other end of the line says, "Do you want him to die?"

I say, "Of course I don't want him to die, I just want to work with him, it would be an honor to work with him."

They say, "No. You're off the film. We are making special compensation for Karloff only. If you show up on the set, we will fine you $2,500 and suspend you for a year."

So I couldn't even visit the set, it really pissed me off."

Pete: Damn, that really sucks.

Sid: Yeah, that's unionism gone bad.

Pete: After *Pit Stop*, you did a big film, *Che!* (1969)

Sid: Che! was an interesting film, as we had advisors who were actually with Castro and Che Guevara. They both said that Che was a monster, an absolute monster. When he finally took power, he had his hit list and he was killing people left and right. Then he wanted to take over Bolivia. I played the leader of the Bolivian communists, Antonio. We were actually supposed to go to Bolivia to shoot this, and I was going to meet the character I was playing, who was in prison there. I was going to get his story. But unfortunately. Malibu Canyon looks exactly like Bolivia, so guess what?

I loved working on the film. Richard Fleischer, an all-time classy director. The year before, he won the Oscar for *Doctor Dolittle.* Very understanding guy. I did a scene at the end where I become disillusioned by Che as a leader. He turned into a total maniac. It was staged with Omar Sharif, who was playing Che, lying in a hammock, and I was standing on a rock looking over him.

We were setting up the scene and I was uncomfortable. To show you how astute Omar was, he said, "Sid, what's wrong?" I said, "Nothing."

He said, "No, what's wrong, what's going on?" It was that my character, Antonio, had so much respect for Che, like a brother, and now he was disillusioned. Omar got it. He said, "Richard, can I see you for a second?" So the director comes over. Omar said "I have an idea." He knew that, coming from me, it wouldn't carry any weight, but coming from him, it would. Omar said, "What if Sid were closer, we start out softly and build it up to when it explodes?"

Richard said, "Damn, you learn something new every day. Let's do it that way." So we reblocked the scene and shot it that way.

Pete: Memories of *Diamonds Are Forever* (1971)?

Sid: That was another great experience. Working with Sean Connery, a great guy, very easy to get along with. No big star attitude, he hated the wig—when a scene wrapped, he'd pull it off and toss it in the air. We got caught up in that whole political thing with Great Britain and

*Sid in **Diamonds Are Forever**.*
(Copyright United Artists. All Rights Reserved.)

Canada about only having so many American actors coming in. The [actors playing The] Slumber Brothers were supposed to go to London, but that got written out. Funny how everyone can come here to work, but we couldn't go there. I hate getting political, but this just pisses me off.

I did *Point Blank* (1967) with Lee Marvin, who was a great guy and I loved hangin' out with him. So I go in for the interview with John Boorman, the director. He wanted to see if I had a feel for the part. So he asked if I was going to be a sniper, what would I do. Well I told him that I would follow the target, get a feel for his patterns. Then set him up—with maybe a car broken down, with the hood up. Then I would dum dum the shell. He asked what I meant by that. I said I would cut a star on the shell, that way it would go in the size of a dime and come out the size of a cash register. Well Boorman loved that line and put it in the film. I didn't get to say it, but it wound up in the film. I had a nice little role. It wasn't big, but it was just cool being with Lee Marvin.

Pete: What was it like hanging out with Lee?

Sid: He got me in three fights in one night. He was, you know, an instigator. At the wrap party, one of the crew was coming on to this girl. Well she wasn't having it, so he threw a shot glass at her. It missed her by a mile, but went whizzing past my head. So Lee says, "Did you see what that guy just did? Are you going to let him get away with that?" So that was fight number one.

Fight number two was another one, I forget how that started, but fight number three was this guy making improper advances to this young lady who was just there to network with people. I told him to knock it off, but he told me to shut up and went back to bothering her. So I threw him against the wall and pinned him there. Later I found out that the guy was Sergio Leone. Then I was never—for some reason (laughing)—cast in a Sergio Leone film.

Pete: I know a lot of actors were going to Italy to do Spaghetti Westerns, did you ever get an offer to go do one?

Sid: I was sort of slated to fall into that Spaghetti western slot as Lee Van Cleef had taken over for Clint Eastwood as the number one guy there. I would have been the number two guy. But the director got nervous because he didn't have the actor he could reach out and touch. Van Cleef was already living there. So because he couldn't sit down and talk with me on a daily basis, he got panicky and hired someone else. But a week after this, Jack Hill called me and said, "I'm going to do a movie in the Philippines, want to come?" So that started my career in the Philippines.

Pete: I know John Ashley did those *Blood Island* films for Hemisphere. I know he had contacted Roger Corman and told him how cheap it was to film there. So I'm guessing Corman contacted Jack Hill, Jack got you.

Sid: Yeah, you're right. The first one was *The Big Doll House* (1971) and that was Pam Grier's first film. Jack said, "We got this girl, she is amazing and I think she'll be a big star." I'm like, "Yeah, OK." Then I met her and found her to be electrifying and she did become a huge star.

We did six films together, *The Big Doll House, The Big Bird Cage* (1972)*, Black Mama White Mama* (1973)*, Coffey* (1973)*, Foxy Brown* (1974), and *Jackie Brown* (1997).

I lived [in the Philippines] for six months, I did four films in six months and became practically a native. It became just like home to me. We were living in the Intercontinental Hotel. Being a kid from the streets, I caught on quick. I got a fistful of five peso notes and took care of people. After that, I never had to lift a finger to do anything. They'd shine my shoes, do my laundry, I had my own table at the coffee shop with a newspaper waiting for me every morning. It was amazing.

Pete: That sounds like head-and-shoulders above the first place you told me you stayed in which was a complete shit hole.

Sid: That was a converted insane asylum. I thought I'd go insane staying there. This guy took me down to a room where all the women went upstairs. They had those old jalousie windows. Mine was missing the bottom pane. When I opened the door, I saw a rat carrying a kitten out the window. It had just killed the kitten and was going to eat it. I said "I don't think so." Then they put me upstairs. That wasn't the best situation either. We had to run the air conditioners all night to keep from being eaten alive by mosquitoes. We had to keep the lights on so we wouldn't be overrun with cockroaches, it was just terrible. Finally, the girls sort of mutinied and were going to leave, so that's how we wound up in the Intercontinental Hotel.

*Sid and Pam Grier in **The Big Doll House.***
(Copyright New World Pictures. All Rights Reserved.)

The Big Doll House was this crazy kind of women-in-prison movie where I played the guy who supplied the prison with produce. But at the same time I was smuggling in mail and other stuff in return for sexual favors. Pam and I had a scene where we were groping each other between the bars, it was a pretty hot little scene. So we staged this crazy break out where I used my produce truck to get them out of prison. It was a crazy film.

In *The Big Bird Cage* I was playing this character called Django, a revolutionary, who was just kind of lazy. We had a group of men and we were going to stage this prison breakout because my men needed the women. So I figured if all these guys were getting laid, the would keep it together and stay in line. At least that was the plan. All of the guards in the prison were gay, so I had to impersonate a gay guy to get hired. When we did this breakout scene, there was a moat surrounding the prison. They were putting rubber cement on a guard to set him on fire. He was supposed to jump in the moat to put it out. So I'm looking in the moat and see a snake in it. I tell a guy there's a snake in the moat. He tells me to shut up or the actor won't jump. So they set him on fire, he jumps into the moat, someone yells 'Snake!' and the guy just about walked on water to get out. That was the kind of stuff we were doing.

The Filipino stunt men were crazy. It was a badge of honor not to wear pads or have airbags. They just fell out of trees and hit the ground. I was supposed to shoot this guy out of a tower. All there was is hard ground. I said I'm not going to do it; the fall was like two stories. I said someone has to get a net. So, reluctantly, they get a net. They have ten guys holding it. I know what was going to happen. They broke the guy's fall, but they had a ten-person head-butt. Now we have bodies all over the ground. At least we saved the guy's life.

Jack Hill sort of created the whole blaxploitation thing with *The Big Doll House, The Big Bird Cage* and now *Coffey*. But Bob Minor couldn't find many black stunt people, so he had to teach people how to throw a punch, how to take a fall, etc. So now we had more work for black actors, more films for black stunt people, and I really think Jack Hill was the guy who really got this thing going for black performers.

I was in *Foxy Brown* too, with Pam and Antonio Fargas. I was playing this whacked-out pilot, crazier than shit. I'm in the plane with Pam and she starts getting "frisky" with me, so I drive the plane into a shack. They had this "stunt" pilot to do this, but for some reason he veered off and the wing took out a $250K camera and gave the operator a black eye. It was a complete mess. They had to get a new camera to finish the film.

Pete: During our little Q&A yesterday, you told a story about running into real head hunters and cannibals.

Sid: Jack had seen pictures of this place, Mount Pulag, the highest point in Luzon. It was beautiful, there were rice paddies cut into the side of the mountain. We were going to go up there and shoot. The only way to get there, because a car ride was 17 hours, was to go by missionary plane that could only take three people at a time. There was no runway, they just shaved the top of the mountain. The pilot came in sideways and sort of just skidded to a stop. A miscalculation would have us fall off the mountain. So Jack, Pam, and I were the last to go up. So we are waiting for our guide, surrounded by jungle and jungle noises, it was pretty cool. So we are going down the trail and I see this little guy, about four feet tall, wearing a loin cloth and carrying a spear. So I tap Pam on the shoulder and say, "Check this out". She took one look and I think she beat everyone to the bottom of the mountain, it was pretty bizarre.

So we are shooting, Jack and I are walking with a guide. The guide tells us that over this hill is a pristine village, but you guys don't want to go there. Well, that an invitation if we ever heard one. So we said, "How do we get there?" He says, "Well, there's a path."

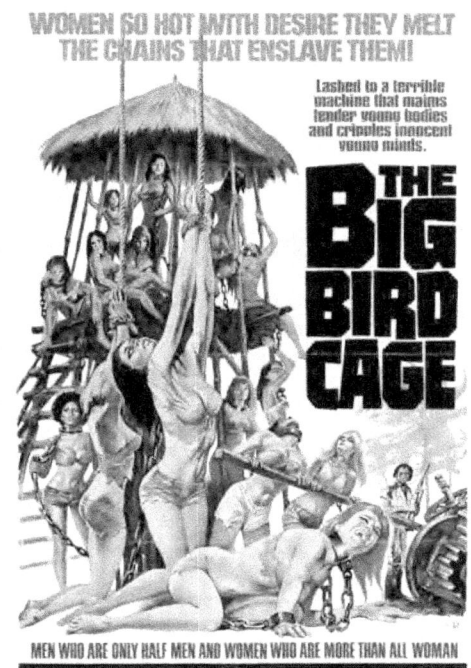

So we get a couple of cameras and take a skeleton crew up the mountain and down the other side. And there it was, a quiet little pristine village. There were little huts surrounding a bigger hut. There was a lot of activity at the bigger one. The guide said it was planting season for the rice. And this was a head hunter's village. He said if contracts aren't honored for the rice, you lose your head. If I say I'm going to marry this guy's daughter and I back out, I lose my head.

So we were there at the right time because they had started planting the rice. So the guide tells us to wait while he sees if it's ok for us to come in. He waves us in, I duck to get into this hut on stilts and come face to face with the chief. Here's this guy, no cartilage in his nose, meat kinda flopping around, one tooth in his head. He hands me this bowl—it's blood with beetle nuts floating around in it. The stuff is like peyote, a hallucinogen.

So I look at the guide and say, "What am I supposed to do with this?" He said to drink it. I said, "C'mon, what are you talking about?" He says, "You *better* drink it."

So I drink it—I find out later that it's chicken blood. Can you spell salmonella? Jack is behind me and he blurts out, "Holy shit!" So I turn to see what he's looking at and the entire eaves of the hut are lined with skulls. Now this is some serious business. So we shot a couple of scenes and the beetle nuts kicked in. I walked seven miles in the jungle, barefoot, and didn't know it. The next day my feet were the size of a couch. I got really fucked up.

Pete: You did a really obscure film called *The Woman Hunt* (1972), any memories of that one?

Sid: It was more than obscure, laughing, maybe six people have seen this film. It was a *Most Dangerous Game* take-off, rich guys hunting down captured women. So they would capture these beautiful women and hunt them down. It was bizarre—they had used horses, but had very small horses over there. I got the biggest horse, but my feet were almost touching the ground. I'd get on, the horse would steady itself, give a loud grunt and pee for a couple of minutes. Then it would get to work. We had a campfire scene, we were all bedded down, then there was this water buffalo laying on its side. Director, Eddie Romero, says to me it would be great if you used the buffalo as a pillow when you go to sleep.

So I'm doing this scene with John Ashley. I throw my coffee away and lay down. Now the buffalo gets up. So we try it a couple of more times and the buffalo keeps getting up. So Eddie asks how do we get him to stay there? [The buffalo's handler] says if I reach back and massage the bull's testicles, he'll stay there. I say, "What?" So I'm one of those guys—whatever it takes to get it done, let's just do it. So there I am, massaging the bull's balls and what really pissed me off was that they cut that shot out of the film. But the bull and I were engaged, laughing.

Pete: You did *Black Mama, White Mama*, a grindhouse-style remake of *The Defiant Ones*—how did that come about?

Sid: I got offered that after *Woman Hunt*. They said there was no point in me going home, then turning around and fly back. So they paid my per diem and kept me in the good hotel. Five weeks later, I'm still there and we haven't filmed a thing. So I called them and asked what the holdup was. They said they hadn't cast the picture. I said, "You know you're going to use Pam Grier, so find a blonde and let's get this thing done."

So the blonde was Margret Markov, who was a year behind me at The Pasadena Playhouse. We knew each other. It became this big family reunion. We had a lot of fun with that film.

Pete: You were really over-the-top in *Savage Sisters* (1974). No Pam Grier, but they brought in Gloria Hendry.

Sid: It was a crazy and I thought how am I going to do this? So I made my character as an homage to Mexican actor Pedro Armendáriz [*Fort Apache, 3 Godfathers*]. So I got the accent down, remember Pedro was the guy who said "Badges? We don't need no stinking badges."[1] So everything I said was *stinking*. 'Stinking this, stinking that.' So at the end when the girls subdued us, they buried me and Vic Diaz up to our necks in sand. So I go off on this diatribe that I chased these stinkin' girls all over this stinkin' island and what do they do? They bury me in this stinkin' sand and piss in my stinkin' face. That was my finale, I thought it was too over-the-top. Eddie Romero said, "No it's really great, let's keep it in."

Pete: Eddie did all those *Blood Island* films, then with you in *Beyond Atlantis* (1973). He had to bring that in with a PG rating.

Sid: Yeah, I think that was because of Patrick Wayne's involvement in the film. He is John Wayne's son, so there wasn't that much over-the-top violence.

Pete: What are your memories of *Beyond Atlantis*?

Sid: That was a very interesting film. The underwater photography was amazing; I mean it was great work. We were filming right were the Bataan Death March took place. In one scene, we are walking through this village and I fall into this booby trap, a pit full of crabs. So I go over where they are digging the pit and it's a hole about two feet deep. I said, "How do you expect me to fall into this? It's crazy." So I ask, "Does anyone know how to dig a grave?" So one guy does. So I say, "Good, make it six feet deep."

So I ask, "Did you spike the claws on the crabs?" They didn't know what I was talking about. You have to stick a sliver of bamboo under the crab's claws so they can't open them. It doesn't hurt the crabs and it prevents them from eating me. So they bring out these two burlap bags full of crabs. It sounded like a flamingo dancer's convention in there because they did not spike the claws. So I tell them to take them back and do what I said to do. It took three days to shoot a scene that should have taken three hours.

---

[1] Sid is thinking of Alfonso Bedoya, who played the infamous bandit "Gold Hat" in *The Treasure of the Sierra Madre* (1948).

Pete: You were paired a lot with resident actor, Vic Diaz. Sometimes you were partners, other times you were at each other's throats. How was it working with Vic?

Sid: Vic was an amazing guy. He was the staple character actor of the country. He played everything from cops to bad guys. He'd play whatever was necessary. He lived through the Second World War. He found this big sack off occupation money as a kid. He thought he was a big hero, but the war was over and the money was worthless. He was funny. He was obnoxious and vulgar, but he came off as really funny.

We were filming on Rojos Blvd—it's a very busy place. All the embassies are on Rojos Blvd; it was known as Embassy Row. We were in front of a casino. Vic turns to Patrick Wayne and says, "Patrick, have you seen the German helmet of Vic Diaz?" So Patrick says no. So Vic whips out his penis, and I say "Vic, put that thing away." Patrick Wayne was flabbergasted; he didn't know what to say. But that was Vic.

We were there to make movies, have fun and if we made a couple of bucks, cool. We had no idea that years down the road that anyone would care about them. If they ran a week or two at the local theater or drive in, we were happy. Some of these just took off and became cult classics. We weren't doing it for the paycheck because the money wasn't there. Believe me when I tell you that.

Pete: Didn't you buy property in the Philippines at one point?

Sid: Yeah, I found this beautiful, peaceful little cove. A friend hooked me up and I got it for $5,000. I enjoyed it for a couple of years. Then Ferdinand Marcos came into power and I lost it. The regime changed a lot of things, and not for the better for the Philippines.

So after that, I go back to Los Angeles and where it sort of rained for like 20 minutes a day in the Philippines, I walked into the smog in LA and my skin actually burned from it. The air is cleaner in the Philippines.

Pete: You also did a lot of TV.

Sid: I did 350 television shows.

Pete: Wow.

Sid: Some were series like *Jason of Star Command* (1978-79) and *Mary Hartman, Mary Hartman* (1976-77), plus I was a regular on several shows. I did nine episodes of *Mission: Impossible* (1966-70) and that was pretty spectacular. I felt great there because of the people I was working with. And I was the only actor to be on that show nine times.

Pete: Memories of *Jason of Star Command?*

Sid: I was playing this Ming the Merciless-type character, Dragos, looming over everyone. Craig Littler was hired to play Jason. We were both the same height, so I was fitted with six-inch platform boots that I wore as part of my costume.

Pete: Didn't they have to make a sort of unique helmet for your character?

Sid: Yeah, I had to come in and they made this helmet which had to be form-fitting. So I lay down on a table, they put this empty paper tube holder in my mouth so I can breathe. Then they mix these two chemicals together and poured it over my head. I looked like I fell asleep under a cow. Then they had to cut it off of me. So the appliance weighed about two pounds. I was part computer, I had a laser beam eye. Then they went to a toy store and bought all these models. They took pieces from the model kits and glued them to the helmet, then painted the whole thing gold. That's how the character was born. This was the most expensive kids' show on the air.

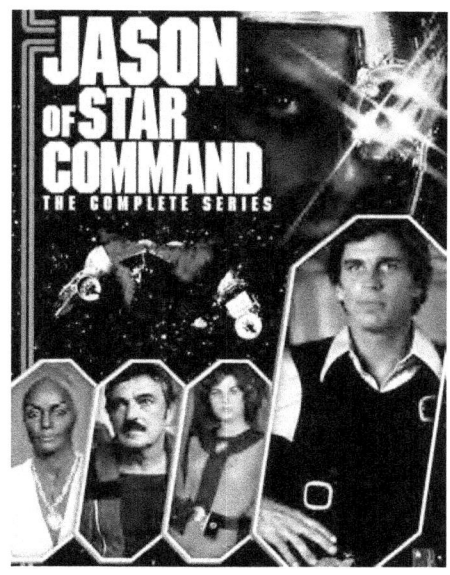

It was a CBS show and it went crazy, we got a 47% share on the ratings. It was doing well, we had 15 episodes, but not 15 scripts. We had only one script. So we had all 15 episodes in one script. We had a five-week shooting schedule to get it all done. So we shoot some in the control room, some in the gangway, etc. You had to keep in your head what episode you were working on. But we were getting it done and everyone was loving the show.

The guy that was head of children's programming at the time, well CBS decided he was entitled to a reward for this great work. So they switched him to nighttime programming. So they give his job to this woman. So she comes down to the set one day with her kid, this rat kid. So I'm walking down the hall to get a cup of coffee or something. So she and her kid turn the corner and her kid walks right into my knee. Well the kid starts crying and the show was cancelled. That was the end of the show because her little booger-eater cried when he ran into me.

Right after that, I was brought in to do *Mary Hartman, Mary Hartman*. It was going to be just one episode. A couple of weeks later they asked me if I wanted to do more. I said yeah, as I had fun doing it. 126 episodes later, they killed me. Actually when I was doing *Mary Hartman,* they wanted me to do *McNamara's Band* (1977)[2] with John Byner. It was a takeoff on *The Dirty Dozen*, really a comedy version of the *Dirty Dozen,* but with just five guys. I wasn't under contract for *Mary Hartman*, I worked independently on the 126 episodes.

So I told them about the pilot, so they said when do you have to do it? I gave them the date, so I had to do all my dialog for the next eleven *Mary Hartman* episodes in one day. I'm doing *McNamara's Band* and the *Mary Hartman* people are calling every half hour. "When is he going to be done, when can we use him?" Stuff like that. So I told them put me in a motel close to the set. Wake me at 8am because I have to be on the set at 9am. I finish *Band* around 2am, now I

---

[2] By all accounts, only the TV-Movie pilot for *McNamara's Band* was ever aired.

*Sid as the Royal Apothecary to Victor Buono's King Tut in the **Batman** TV series.*
(Copyright 20th Century Fox Television. All Rights Reserved.)

*Sid in one of his appearances on **Get Smart!***
(Copyright CBS Productions. All Rights Reserved)

need sleep to wind down from that. I go to the studio and find out that I have to do five episode's worth of dialog in one day to get them back on schedule. It was brutal

Pete: A lot of your stuff would be classified as grindhouse drive-in films. Two that stand out were a couple of biker films. You played Pillbox in *Trained to Kill, USA* (aka *The No Mercy Man,* 1973) and you were in *C.C. and Company* (1970) with Joe Namath.

Sid: I was prepared not to like Joe Namath because I had this thing about pro athletes walking into starring roles in films. You know they come in with no training, have egos, shit like that. But Joe was such a charming guy that I couldn't get pissed at him. It was a cool film to work on because I knew Bill [William Smith] and Ann Margret was such a sweetheart, her husband was the producer and things went smoothly.

Pete: I remember you telling me about an incident after hours, you and Bill Smith went into a bar in costume.

Sid: When you're working in the Southwest, it's hot and there's a lot of dust and dirt in the air. It winds up in your throat. So the first thing Bill and I would do after shooting was to go to the hotel bar and down a few long necks to cut the dust. We were always in 'wardrobe" and wardrobe was a little stale, like we smelled like dead goats. The bartender was used to us coming in and had the beer ready. So one day this guy in a three-piece suit is next to me. He has no idea what we are doing and blurts out, "Why the hell did you guys come in here?" So Bill reaches across me, grabs this guy by the throat and tells him, "We're selling tickets to an ass kicking, you want one?" The guy threw all kinds of money on the bar and ran out.

Another night, we get a little tipsy, We decide to break into the trailer, grab a couple of bikes and go for a ride. We didn't, though, because we would have wound up dead. But Bill and I always had a great time together.

Pete: Didn't you do an episode of *Wildside* (1985) with Bill?

Sid: *Wildside* was sort of Disney, it didn't last a season. [Wrestler] Terry Funk was in it, great guy. He'd tear your head off in a wrestling ring, but otherwise wouldn't hurt a fly. It didn't have a real lot going for it. It had some young guys who were new, but good-looking kids. It was a shame because Bill was really good in it. It just didn't catch on with viewers.

Pete: Something a lot of people don't know is that you appeared in two Bob Hope Christmas Specials.

Sid: No one was more surprised about that than me. I was with my family and I was supposed to pick up a script at CBS studios. We went to a restaurant, I left the family there, grabbed the script and came back. There are two guys there that don't look like they have two nickels to rub together. Unshaven, clothes rumpled, etc. So one guy turns to me and says, "Are you an actor? What's your name?" So I tell him. I give him my agent's name.

The guys say, "We are writing skits for the new Bob Hope Christmas Special and you'd be perfect for a role in one of the skits that he's doing." I'm like, 'OK, heard all this before.'

So [my family and I] go off to do what we have to do. I get home and there's a message from my agent. "They want you for the
Bob Hope Special. They want you for the job". That really drove home the 'don't judge a book by its cover thing,' like I did with these two guys.

And what was so cool about it was that I had just done *Point Blank* with Lee Marvin. Lee was also in the same Bob Hope Special. Lee is like me, he likes to get to the set early. I walk on stage for rehearsal and Lee is there reading a newspaper. He looks up and says "Sid, how are you doing?" I was like, what a memory, it's been four years. It was just great working with him again.

Bob Hope was very nice to me. We were done rehearsing and he says "What are you doing now?" I say, 'just hanging around,' so he invites me back to his dressing room. A guy makes us a couple of drinks and we shoot the breeze for like 20 minutes. Then he had to talk to some people, so I excused myself and let. He was a very gracious man.

Pete: You did another film with Lee, *Emperor of the North Pole* (1973), also with Ernest Borgnine. That fight scene was pretty brutal, how much of it was stunt men and how much of it was Lee and Ernie?

Sid: Part of it was them and part of it was stunt men. But yeah, it was a great fight scene. Both great guys to work with. The hobo camp scene, where Lee steals a turkey and hands it off to me, well the camera man yells to me, "Sid, the turkey's head is blocking your face." So I hypnotized it, put my finger on its head, and yelled to the camera man, 'Tell me when the shot is good.' It worked, turkeys are stupid.

Pete: Memories of *Trained to Kill, USA* aka *The No Mercy Man*?

Sid: We shot that in Patagonia ,Arizona, which was 26 miles from the Mexican border. Small town, maybe 400 people. We heard later that they shipped all the women under 30 out of the town while we were making the film. They thought these Hollywood types are crazy and are going to rape our women. It was just nuts. It was a rural area; they had a town marshal and a

federal marshal. Paul Sorenson was the federal marshal and he was so good at what he did, marksmanship-wise. Firing 2000 rounds, only four wound up out of the black, the bullseye. That was impressive. So impressive that when Queen Elizabeth came here to visit, she requested Paul to be on her security team.

So here he is in this small border town. We became friends and we are having dinner one night. He gets a call at the front desk. There's a fight at THE bar—yeah, it was THE bar, THE Gas Station, THE hotel, etc. So he says, "Keep my food warm, I'll be back in a couple of minutes." He is back in two minutes. I said, "I know you're the tough guy in town, but you just broke up a fight, put them in jail, and you're back here in two minutes?"

He says "You are from the city, ain't you? I walked in, pulled out my club, knocked them both out and it will be a month before they try to do that again".

Pete: Oddly some of the films you have done have sort of disappeared thought the cracks. *Busting!* (1974) was one of them.

Sid: Yeah, that was cool. I've never seen it, never. I wanted to work with these guys, Robert Blake and Elliot Gould. So when I get there, they had been filming for a couple of days. So I say my lines and someone starts talking. So I say, "Excuse me, are there any pages that I didn't get, did I miss something?"

"No," they said. "We threw that script away a week ago." So most of that film was improvising. The skeleton of the script was there—like, this has to happen, that has to happen, but the dialogue, 90% was improvised.

Robert Blake, for the whole time I was doing this film, wouldn't talk to me, wouldn't even say hello in the morning. So I'm thinking this guy is a little asshole. We are done filming. A couple of weeks later, I'm in Hollywood and at a stoplight, there's a car behind me honking the horn. I'm thinking, 'What a jackass! I'm at the stop light.' So out of the car jumps Bobby Blake, he runs up to me and says "How are ya doing? It's great to see you." Then I got it, Blake was such a method actor that he wouldn't break character until the film wrapped.

Pete: You were telling me about something going wrong with a blood squib when they shot you at the end.

Sid: Oh! [laughing] No, I actually shot myself. They set it up with a little aluminum foil on my head, then covered it with mortician's wax and ran the wire down the back of my neck and down my arm. It went to the gun I was holding so that when I pulled the trigger, the squib would go off. So basically I was shooting myself in the head.

Pete: You were in *Galaxy of Terror* for Roger Corman's New World Pictures, I think it was '81 or '82.

Sid: It was '81. Roger Corman wanted me to do this. I said 'I'll do this on one condition.' He said, "You're not getting any more money."

I said, 'I don't want any more money, I want to do it silent. You know, mute."

He says, "Why?" I said, "Have you read that shit?"

He says "Oh, yeah, OK, do it silent."

So I did it silent, except that director made me say that stupid line, "I live and die by the crystals." Please! [Laughing]

Pete: What are your thoughts on Roger Corman?

Sid: Roger is the greatest movie genius that there is. He is the best at making and marketing films. He taught me—and he doesn't know this—he taught me everything I know about marketing. He's a genius when it comes to that. We were doing a film called *Wizards of the Lost Kingdom, Part II* (1989). There was no Part One. He said if the film worked, we could make part one and release it "due to popular demand." Everything he does has that stamp of something different on it.

Hollywood is a place that will typecast you immediately. If you do a credible job, say as a bank robber, you'll be playing bank robbers for the rest of your life. It got so bad with me, that I had had it. I just flipped Hollywood off. If you guys can't figure out that I can do more than just stick a gun in someone's face, then I'm through. I just walked away in 1992.

Well I had to do something for a living and I was doing a lot of self-studies in psychology to develop my characters, so that was the field I was looking into. But I couldn't go back to school for ten years to be a psychiatrist. So I found the Hypnosis Motivation Institute. It was the only accredited college of hypnotherapy in the country. So I applied, I went down and took a test to prove that I'm not nuts—because you'll be working with other people. So I wasn't nuts. I enrolled and at the age of 58, I took out a student loan and went back to school. About 1,700 hours of instruction, I did my internship, and then started my practice. Everything was going smooth, then Quentin Tarantino called me.

He called me at home, who knows how he got my phone number. He said, "I know you don't want to play stupid heavies, but I've written this role for you. You play a judge and I won't take no for an answer."

So I'm like, "OK, boss." So there I am in *Jackie Brown* as a judge.

Pete: And we heard that Pam Grier didn't know that you were going to be there and she lost her shit when she walked onto the set.

Sid: On purpose he did not tell Pam that he cast me. She literally hit the floor. We hadn't seen each other in like 27 years. It was like we just had lunch the day before, the relationship just picked back up. We had fun and Quentin Tarantino is the complete movie buff. All during the film, he kept quoting lines from every movie that I had ever done. I said "How do you remember all this shit? I don't even remember what I said."

Pete: You said you got offered four different roles in *Kill Bill*?

Sid: I don't know what the deal was there. I was supposed to be the orderly who was pimping the unconscious girl, Uma Thurman. Then somebody else got that role. Then he gave me another role, somebody else got that. So then I got the bartender [*Kill Bill Volume 2,* in the bar where Michael Madsen's character works], which was fine. I just wanted to work with him because he's so cool to work with.

I got a call from my agent who I hadn't heard from for a long time. He said, "I have a deal for you."

I said, "What deal?"

He said, "You go to this office on Wilshire Blvd, you sign a non-disclosure statement, you get a script, take it home and if you like it, the part is yours."

*With Pam in **Jackie Brown**.*
(Copyright Miramax Films. All Rights Reserved.)

I said, "OK, well somebody's got it right."

So I picked up this script for *House of 1000 Corpses*. So I took it home and read it. I said to myself I could really have fun with this, it's completely crazy. So I said yes, I really want to do this. So there you go, my career got started all over again.

I likened the film to *The Wild Bunch*. It was rough, it was raw, and brutal at times. I thought it was a really good script and I wanted to do it. So after we filmed it, I got a call from Rob. He said, "I can't really talk now, but I have a reporter here from Variety and he wants to know if I do a sequel, will you be in it?" I said "Definitely." And that's how *The Devil's Rejects* was born.

Pete: That film had one hell of an ensemble cast. I said once before that everyone tries to make an ensemble cast movie, but it only works if the audience feels for the characters. You get to know the characters, actually care about them and feel bad when they die. I mean you, Bill Mosely, and Sherri Moon get shot to pieces at the end, and the audience was visibly upset by that.

Sid: People have told me that they cried at the end of that film. There was a turning point in the film where people actually started siding with us. It was the ice cream eating scene. I know there were people thinking that my family would also argue about ice cream. At that point, they all were on our side.

Pete: Let me ask you something about your costars. There were so many great people involved. Let me throw out a couple of names: Michael Berryman.

Sid: Michael is such a cool guy and he played that role perfectly, a simple dunce, stumbling through life and doing whatever Ken Foree told him to do.

Pete: Bill Mosely, your son/costar or whatever he was supposed to be.

Sid: He wasn't my son; in the biography we were in jail together. When we got out, we staged a couple of unsuccessful bank robberies. So I took off, he stayed at the Firefly Ranch and became the patriarch of all the wackos. Both women [who played "Mama Firefly], Karen Black and Leslie Easterbrook, had their own takes on the character and both were right for what they were. I personally liked Leslie's take on it better. She was this hard-assed woman lording over this houseful of crazies. She took a lot of shit and gave it all back. I thought she did an excellent job.

Pete: How about the two bounty hunters, Danny Trejo and Diamond Dallas Page?

Sid: I love Danny, he's a great guy. And Diamond and I get along really well. The 2nd Spike TV Scream Awards, Danny Trejo and I were presenters. The way we would pick out the winner was this Plexiglas box with the envelope in it. They wanted Danny to pick out the winner. The thing was that the box was full of Emperor Scorpions. Danny says "I'm not putting my hand in there."

I say "Danny, don't worry about it, they are Emperors. They're not poisonous.

He looked at me and said, "Why does everybody think that Mexicans are stupid?" So I stuck my hand in and they all scattered when I picked up the envelope.

Pete: Bill Forsythe, who played the sheriff, actually wound up being the bad guy in the film.

Sid: Bill works very much like I do. Sometimes he's a loose cannon, which is OK because that brings another dimension to the character. It was good working with him.

Pete: Sherri Moon

Sid: Sherri is a sweetheart, a genuinely nice person. I love her; she's like my own daughter. *House* was her first film. When we did the table

The Devil's Rejects: *Sid, Sherri Moon (Baby), Matt McGrory (Tiny), Leslie Easterbrook (Mama), Bill Moseley (Otis). Copyright Lionsgate.*

read, she was sitting across from me and I could feel the heat coming off her body as she was so nervous being in a room full of accomplished actors. Karen Black sort of took her under her wing, calmed her down and helped her get into her role. So by the time we did Rejects, she was really rockin' it.

Pete: Matt McGrory.

Sid: Matt was such a nice guy and left us way too early.

Pete: I met him once at a convention, he was a really nice person, but seemed to be in a lot of pain.

Sid: Terrible pain daily. 24/7 in pain. It's such a sad story because he met this girl, they fell in love. She moved out to California to be with him. She came home from work one day and found him dead. It was a very sad time for all of us—we loved Matt, he was just great.

Pete: I first met you at the Chiller Theatre Convention. Four or so years prior to that I kept asking, "Why don't we try to find Sid Haig, he'd be great here?" Then bang, you come in, you break the bank and also find the love of your life.

Sid: Yep, we were called into this place, Gentle Giant, to get full body scans done for action figures. I said what? Action figures? So I stood on this platform and they scanned me and through a computer, it turned a block of foam into *you*. So I was thinking about this whole 15-minutes-of-fame stuff. I thought I better make this work. I was friends with Eric Caiden of

Hollywood Book & Poster and asked him how this convention stuff worked. Then I asked if he could get me into one and did he think I could do something there.

So he said, "Yeah, no problem," and he got me into Chiller, which was the huge horror convention at the time. *House of 1,000 Corpses* had just been released, so I came in not knowing what to expect. I had this huge line of people that wanted to meet me, have a picture taken with me and buy whatever I was selling, it was crazy. So I said yeah, I have to keep doing these.

I was talking to this girl on my message board. Well at Chiller she walked into the room and now she's my wife. She has done so much for me, not only as a person, but as an actor. I'm totally amazed and in love with what she is.

Pete: After that, you sort of exploded. You did two Chillers, and like ten MonsterManias, and you sort of put that show on the map. Now we are back here to a huge response at Saturday Nightmares.

Sid: It's amazing. Sometimes I don't get it, but I am certainly not going to snub my nose at it. The fans are the most amazing people around. Horror film fans, they are the best. They are there for you all the time. They buy the tickets, the DVDs, the T-shirts, they support everything that you do. I love 'em, man, they are the best.

This is the message I try to give to everybody, I don't care what it is that you do, try to make it fun. Try to make anything you do fun. Because if you're having fun with it, you're doing it well. Now it's something that's joyous, it's not labor. Just have fun with what you are doing.

In the 51 years that I have been doing this, I had to reinvent myself at least four times. When I was doing all that television, it was 'Jesus, no we've seen enough of Sid Haig.' So I'd have to back off and start over again. So I've restarted my career at least four or 5 times. But I like what I do, and it's worth going through a little bit of pain to get the gain. The typecasting comes into play again because I do a lot of horror. But I'm doing other things too.

I did something called *A Dead Calling* (2006) where I played a straight-up Norman Rockwell dad—and people were pissed off about that because I didn't kill anybody! [Shaking his head] I did a film called *Mimesis* (2011), about a filmmaker at a convention doing a panel. I was a psychiatrist in *The Inflicted* (2012) Even though I'm still in the horror genre, I'm spreading out and doing different kinds of things. The last film I just did was *Zombex* (2013), where I play the commander of a special forces unit.

Pete: How do you feel about these films that had you in them for maybe 10 minutes, they throw your name on the DVD cover as the "star" of the film?

Sid: That's merchandising, I have become in the ultra-low budget film business, the poster child for horror. I don't like the idea that, and I hate to get into this thing but I will, the perception is that they can't afford to have me in the entire film, but they want me there for marketing purposes. I get a minor role, they do all my scenes in one day, and get me out, because all they can afford me for is one day. They should get it together with the financing and give me more time so it would be more legitimate to have me on the cover.

Pete: So where do these guys make their mistakes with these films?

Sid: You have to engage the audience; you have to make them care about the characters. Look what Rob Zombie did with these sociopaths, the Fireflies. He made the audience care about them. That's what it's all about, you have to study film. You can't just go buy a camera and say I'm a director. It's crazy, it's like someone going out and buying a scalpel and saying I'm a doctor. You have to get your audience before you make your film, that's the way it works now.

Pete: If you had your dream project, what would it be?

Sid: OK, I'll get political.

Pete: No problem, go for it

Sid: I feel the need and responsibility to make a film around the Armenian Holocaust. It was the first holocaust of the 20th century, it was brutal, mean and vicious. I just feel that this story needs to get told. It's part of my culture in the same way that the Jewish Holocaust is part of Steven Spielberg's culture. I'm not comparing myself to Spielberg, but he had a passion for that and I have a passion for this. I just want to get it done.

Career-wise, I would have liked to have a career like Brando did, like Olivier did. And the reason I'm saying this is because they had a wide variety of roles that they played. When it comes down to it, I think the only genre I have not touched is romance. I have regrets about some of the things that have gone on. I have to take a true evaluation as to what's been going on, and for most of my life, I was in second place.

I have never been in first place. I would really like to be there someday. I just keep working and maybe someday I'll get there.

Pete: What advice would you give someone trying to get into the business besides "don't quit your day job?" (Both of us laughing}

Sid: Just be sure you want to do it. There are a lot of hardships. You can't be thin skinned. If you are, get a retail job. This business is brutal. I've done all this film and TV work, been on 2,000 interviews, so you have to get used to people saying "no." And if that crushes you, you're probably in the wrong business. You have to be tough, you have to be passionate about what you are doing and be willing to starve. I know that's and old cliché, but it's not a cliché, it's the truth. There are a lot of lows and down time in my career.

I was living in a dormitory and we had little lockers to put our food in. So one night I open it and all I had was a box of rice. So I pick it up and there's maybe a spoonful left in it. So that's all I had to eat. But I didn't quit, you can't quit. This brings me to something that I have said before, never quit. My friend, David Carradine, said that there are no failures in Hollywood, only people who quit too soon.

This past year, I received an Eyegore Award from Universal Studios. They knew a horror actor would never get an Academy Award, so they came up with the Eyegores. Rob Zombie presented me with a Lifetime Achievement Award, it couldn't have been a bigger highlight. So I counted and reflected all my struggle, getting my first job, then my second job, then trying to get more money, then trying to get better roles. Then after 50 years, maybe a little respect. That's it.

Pete: I would think that you have that right about now

Sid: If that's true, I'm just so appreciative of it. Sometimes it makes me speechless, I mean people would stop by my table and say things that are so flattering that I don't know how to respond. The only way I can respond is to say thank you. As far as I'm concerned, I haven't gotten there yet. I haven't earned my own respect, let's put it that way. When people start to respect what you've done, it is a motivator because people are paying attention. Thank you, I'll move on and do better the next time.

Pete: Well, here's hoping for another 50 years.

***

All I can add is that I hope he is at peace. We were all devastated by his passing, but anyone who ever met Sid walked away with a good feeling, Sid, I know I'll see you in the hereafter, and save a seat for me at the bar. *Vaya con dios*, my friend.

a Brief elegy for movie Star Sid Haig

by Dr. Rhonda Baughman

It's 2020 now and the idea of the movie star is a fading, flickering ideal. A vague, abstract concept at best. I recently read People/Star/US Weekly magazines while in a stupidly long line at the grocery check out and I was unable to recognize 75% of the "stars" in it[4]. Most folks in those mags are certainly not what I would consider "movie stars"[5]. I define "movie star" these days as someone recognizable based on their talent, their screen presence—someone who has a career I'm jealous of (that is, their resume has movie listed on it that I would kill the neighbors to be in!). A movie star is someone who is accessible to fans and generates a positive buzz at autograph tables. A movie star is someone who brings their A—game to every project, even when they might have felt like shit. The movie star is someone who gives the industry a part of himself even when the industry doesn't deserve it. Finally, a movie star has no time, no patience for trolls and bullshittery. I've set the bar high for movie star expectations, I know. I didn't know Sid personally, but I have a few good friends who did—and one thing I can say with certainty is that Sid was a movie star as I defined it.

Haig was a convention fan favorite, too—tirelessly on the circuit, and a gentleman who

---

[3] Photograph copyright unknown. All rights reserved by original rights holder.

[4] Seriously, who the fuck even *are* most of these people? Are they real?

[5] And hell yes, you bet I hear that phrase, "I'm a movie star," in the voices of Taissa Farmiga and Malin Akerman from *The Final Girls* (2015).

interviewed like a boss and dispensed advice to those who asked—and he acted for over 50 years! 50 fuckin' years! Didn't he make us laugh!? Wasn't he fuckin' funny!? Did you hear those previous two sentences in his voice? Because I know I did. Now to me, that's a movie star! If you can hear someone's voice on the TV, and from another room know exactly who it is after one line—that's a damn movie star. He acted longer than I've acted. Hell, he acted longer than I've been on the planet. That's a movie star!

As 2019 rolled into 2020, I popped in my *Women in Cages Collection*, watching Haig in both *The Big Bird Cage* (1972) and *Big Doll House* (1971)—I could tell he wanted to be there, on set. I could tell he enjoyed being there, on set. There's genuine love and camaraderie on that screen, between Haig and his co—stars. I can see it. Those of you reading this—so could you. It's something special that can't be faked. And in the end, there was more love than hate, more fans who rallied than trolled when they saw Haig had taken ill, and generations of fans who were saddened to hear a screen legend was gone.

And that screen legend, Sid Haig, was a true icon. Not the absolute final, but definitely—he was one of the last original masters standing in the horror and exploitation genres. Not an Academy Award winner, but he was nominated for and had been selected for other awards: Eyegore, Chainsaw, IFS, Sitges, Scream, among plenty others—and Haig is not relegated to obscure *that guy* status either. He left us at age 80. Of course he did—the number 8 is in there. And like the 8—the symbol for infinity—Sid Haig is forever.

Pam and Sid. Copyright New World Pictures. All Rights Reserved.

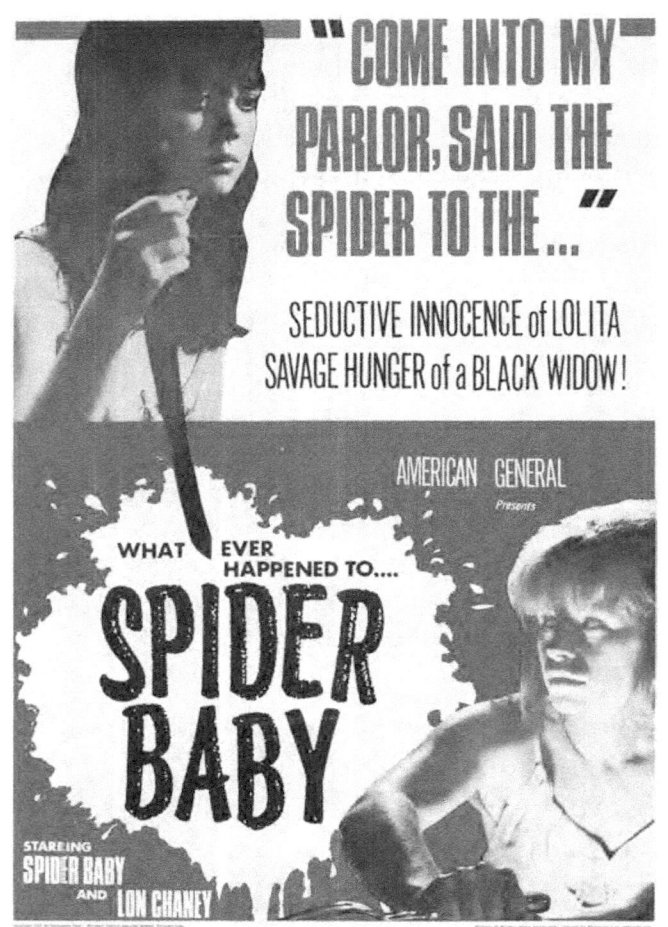 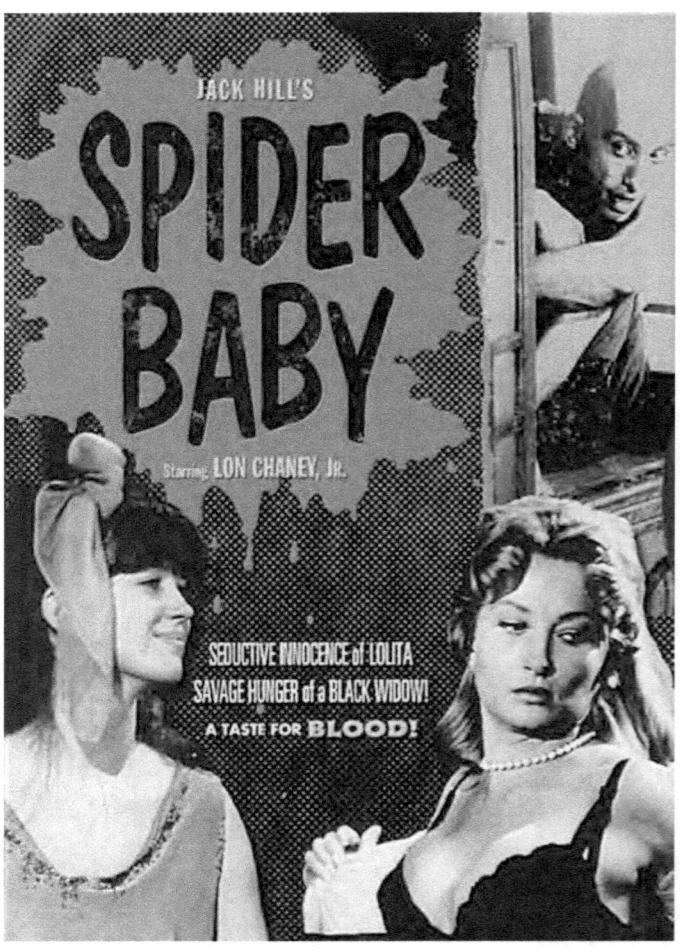

Spider Baby, or The Maddest Story Ever Told (1967)

By David Phillips

"'Will you walk into my parlour?' said the Spider to the Fly."
- *The Spider and the Fly,* by Mary Howitt.

    An actor can't achieve more in the Exploitation genre than Sid Haig. He was in movies with Pam Grier. He appeared in *Savage Sisters*, a women-in-prison movie from 1974. *Savage Sisters* was shot in the Philippines. In the Grindhouse scene it would be hard to top those credits. Haig will be remembered by fans for any number of parts he's played. When I learned that this issue of *Grindhouse Purgatory* was going to be devoted to Sid Haig my mind went to one movie: *Spider Baby*. My relationship with it is one of the maddest stories of me exploring the genre.
    I vividly remember seeing *Spider Baby* for the first time a few years ago. It was available to stream for free through one of the services on my Smart TV. The title had intrigued me for years, and it was on my list of classics I hadn't yet seen. I had questions about it. Who or what was the Spider Baby? Was there even a Spider Baby in the movie, or was the title designed to generate interest before the movie pulled the rug from under me? What's with the subtitle *The Maddest Story Ever Told*? As I hovered over the icon for *Spider Baby* on the TV that day, I decided it was

time I get some answers. The only thing I knew is that it was written and directed by the legendary Jack Hill, and starred Gilbert Gottfried's favorite actor, Lon Chaney, Jr. [If you aren't listening to Gilbert Gottfried's movie podcast, check it out. Guests he's had on include Roger Corman, Joe Dante, and Tom Savini.]

Spider Baby was Jack Hill's first feature film. He would go on to write and direct *Coffy* (1973), and *Foxy Brown* (1974). Hill came from the Roger Corman school of directing along with Francis Ford Coppola, Peter Bogdanovich, Joe Dante, and Ron Howard. Not an actual school for film making, "the Corman school" meant you'd work for Corman and he'd give you your first break. Corman would tell people if they worked for him and did a good job, they'd never have to work for him again. On the last day of filming *The Terror* (1963), Jack Nicholson asked Corman if he could direct because all of the other actors already had a turn during the film's production.

There must have been a lot going on in Jack Hill's mind when he wrote *Spider Baby*. It was originally named *Cannibal Orgy or, the Maddest Story Ever Told*, a play on the title *The Greatest Story Ever Told*. *Spider Baby* had a budget of $65,000. Hill shot it in 16 days in 1964, but it wasn't released until 1967 because the producers, real estate developers, went bankrupt and had their assets seized. The plot in one sentence: A man named Bruno is the guardian of the Merrye siblings, two girls and a boy born with a degenerative condition that causes them to regress mentally. What this means to the viewer is that the siblings look like young adults while behaving like children. This caused a few minutes of confusion for me, which I enjoyed, when I saw the movie the first time. As the film begins, the mental condition of the siblings hasn't been revealed to us, and the two girls come across as childish and, well, kinda sexy for their age.

*Sid and Mantan Moreland in **Spider Baby**.*
(All photos this section copyright American General Pictures. All Rights Reserved)

As the movie opens, Virginia, the Spider Baby of the film's title, has just "caught a fly," a delivery man trapped in the window of her house. Virginia is obsessed with spiders, and sees an opportunity to "sting" the man to death with a knife in each hand. I wondered how old the character was supposed to be, and I wondered how old the actress was. Virginia was played by Jill Banner, who was 17 when *Spider Baby* was filmed. It's obvious that's she's stunning, and you can't take your eyes off of her.

Virginia's sister Elizabeth enters the room, and doesn't seem particularly rattled by the corpse draped over the window sill. Virginia, also beautiful with her short hair in pigtails, was played by Beverly Washburn, 21 at the time of filming, and already an accomplished actress. So the movie is already wonderfully-strange. We have a Lolita type who has just killed a man, and her sister who's acting as if she's seen this before. The behavior doesn't match the appearance of the two young women. A Duesenberg pulls up to the house, and we are introduced to Bruno, the caretaker played by Lon Chaney Jr., who approaches the porch and sees the body of the dead man. The camera cuts to Virginia who is now playfully skipping rope. Jill Banner truly understood her character, and uses every shot she's in to be both dangerous and flirtatious. Elizabeth explains the situation to Bruno: "I didn't do it. She did. She was playing spider. You should hate her." Virginia runs to the car excited to see her brother Ralph, the last of the siblings we meet. Ralph appears to be suffering from the condition more than his sisters, and has the mannerisms of an infant. He's tall, has no hair, can't speak, and his face is sometimes contorted as if there's something he's trying to say. I looked at Ralph's face and it hit me - "Is that...a young Sid Haig?" A quick search online confirmed my guess. Haig was 25 years old when *Spider Baby* was filmed, and already had a respectable list of acting credits. He shaved his head to play Ralph, and doesn't have his signature scruffy beard we're used to seeing today. I was shocked when he appears in the movie because I had no idea he was in it.

Bruno is a real gentle giant who never gets angry. He has his hands full looking after the three siblings, and reminds Virginia, "I promised your father I'd never hate you." Bruno learns that they are going to have visitors at the house later that day, so he and Ralph remove any evidence of the delivery man being there. Ralph hides the man's scooter while Bruno ditches the body.

The visitors arrive. They are Aunt Emily and Uncle Peter who are interested in becoming the new legal guardians of the children. They are met at the house by a lawyer, Schlocker, and his assistant, Ann. The mental condition of the siblings is revealed to us as Bruno explains to his guests that the children are regressing from a condition caused by years of inbreeding. Exactly how much of the disease controls their actions? Exactly how repressed are they? Banner and Washburn are cast perfectly, and spend a lot of the movie's running time giving performances of seductress' trapped inside the bodies of young women. They seem, most of the time, to be well aware that they have the ability to seduce and/or manipulate anyone who looks at them, including the viewers of the movie. They can quietly express themselves by cutting their eyes a certain way, and I think this shorthand is responsible for a big part of the movie's success. I imagine the two actresses practicing their expressions off camera to pin down the exact look when needed.

The performance by Sid Haig is in the complete opposite direction. His character, Ralph, isn't going to seduce anyone. But first, here's a thought: I have a rule that an actor should never play a mentally challenged part in a movie (unless the actor *is* mentally challenged) for two reasons: 1) It comes across as cringe inducing, insulting, and embarrassing. See Rosie O'Donnell in *Riding the Bus With My Sister*, or Juliette Lewis and Giovanni Ribisi in *The Other Sister*. Now that I think about it, don't see those. And my second reason is: Once I see an actor trying to play a mentally challenged person, I will always see them as mentally challenged. It's impossible for me to look at Giovanni Ribisi's face and not see him as a little slow. That's not my fault—he played the part, and the connection has been made. But back to Sid Haig. His performance as Ralph is completely believable and fearless. Ralph is sometimes scary, and other times lovable. If you were in a room with Ralph would you really be in any danger? Haig based his performance on the non-filtered honest reactions of primates and children. Ralph seems to be studying anything that moves or makes a sound. Haig plays the part without any dialog as he would do years later in *Galaxy of Terror*.

Bruno is rattled when the guests insist on spending the night at the house and staying for dinner, but optimistically assures them that something can be found to eat. You wonder why anyone would insist on spending the night in this house. Aunt Emily turns out to be a gold digger, and she seems to think the house is already hers. Schlocker assures her that she has a "*Prima facie* open and shut case." *Prima facie* is a Latin expression for "based on first impression, or accepted as correct until proved otherwise."

Dinner is served after Ralph was kind enough to catch something. Virginia has picked mushrooms. Bruno tells the guests to take a seat at the table, and look at this—

Ralph has cleaned himself up for dinner. He joins the guests wearing a hat and a jacket, shirt and shorts he outgrew years ago. Haig said he felt "stupid" wearing the outfit according to the commentary track on the DVD. The scene at the dinner table is one of the movie's highlights. It runs over eight minutes and could have been a boring disaster in a different movie. The scene moves well thanks to the dialog by Hill and the lighthearted performances of the actors.

Uncle Peter incorrectly assumes that Ralph caught a rabbit. Whatever it is, only the guests will be eating Ralph's catch after Bruno explains the diet of the children: "The eating of flesh would hasten the progress of their condition." It's interesting that Bruno uses the word "flesh" instead of "meat." The lines, "We're vegetarians," and "It's dead. We don't eat dead things," must have been interesting when the movie was released in 1967. Protein powders, diet shakes, and The Grapefruit Diet were around then, but Bruno saying that he and the children are vegetarians seems out of place in the Merrye House. There are other dishes available for those who passed on Ralph's catch, and Bruno delivers the beautiful line, "If you don't feel up to the heavier fare, perhaps you'd like to try some of our fresh garden greens?" He is referring to a pile of what appears to be tumbleweeds sitting in a bowl on the table. Bruno warns that the guests wouldn't want to eat the dish that Virginia prepared for herself. Aunt Emily decides to skip all of the offerings, and angrily opens a bag of potato chips she had in her handbag. Have you ever gone to a restaurant and left hungrier than when you arrived because the over-priced portions were so small? That's what this dinner scene feels like, minus the over-priced part.

A series of scenes that take place after dinner reveal various secrets hidden in the Merrye House. Schlocker thinks there's something funny going on, and with the enthusiasm of a criminal in a *Scooby Doo* cartoon, promises to figure out what. Sid Haig gets a moment to shine when the script needs Ralph to peek through a window and watch Emily as she's undressing. Emily, played by Carol Ohmart, gets a moment to shine by undressing. She was thoughtful enough to wear a black bra and classic stockings with garters that day. The camera stays on her as she twirls around in front of a mirror. Hey, this is Exploitation. The scene is perfect for Ohmart, who started her career as a model. She had already played the 1950's temptress-type in movies prior to *Spider Baby*. You may have seen her in *House on Haunted Hill* (1959).

Virginia is in another memorable scene after she catches Uncle Peter in a web, sits in his lap, and asks if he likes spiders. She playfully tosses her skirt around and asks, "Do you like...me?"

Peter gets the feeling he might possibly be in danger, and plays along with her as best he can. It's fascinating to watch the two actors work with the material and each other. The movie is almost over by this point. It doesn't overstay its welcome, and *Spider Baby* ends with both a bang, and a teaser.

Spider Baby is an enjoyable and wild ride. If you haven't seen it in a while, it might be time to watch it again as we remember Sid Haig. It's a movie that gets better on repeated viewings, and is an example of how great a low-budget movie can be when everyone involved cares to do their best. Jack Hill started the production with a script that is dark, funny, clever, and contains beautiful dialog. Exterior shots were carefully composed to make the Merrye House appear to be the only building around for miles when in reality it was on a block with other homes. Available light was used to shoot some interior shots, and there's a story on the DVD about how the cinematographer, Alfred Taylor, used a trail of reflectors to bounce light from outside the house to the inside when there was no electricity. The score was written by Ronald Stein, who previously provided music for movies by Roger Corman, and other directors. The score fits the tone of the movie perfectly, and Stein made decisions like using a xylophone for moments to tell the audience they aren't in too much danger. Stein knew how to get a lot for the money, and went to Mexico to record the music for *Spider Baby* for $2,500. If it's 1964 and you have $65,000 to make a movie, you want all the money to wind up on screen without the actors complaining about the size of their trailers.

Spider Baby was one of the last movies Lon Chaney Jr. appeared in before he died in 1973. I think he gives, by far, the best performance of his career in this film. Haig remembered that Chaney Jr. was excited that people still knew who he was when the movie was made. I can imagine he'd feel that way in 1964. I'm sure thousands of people in the history of the movies would be amazed today if they knew their work was alive through the Internet, home video and TVs with the aspect-ratios of movie screens.

Jill Banner's life was cut short when she died in a car accident in 1982 at age 35. She was in a relationship with Marlon Brando at the time after the two met on the set of *Candy* (1968). She has fifteen acting credits on IMDb, but will always be remembered in the cult film *Spider Baby*.

I was at a Horror convention in 2015 and the line to meet a guest ran across the floor of the celebrity room and spilled down the length of a hallway. "Who's this line for?" I asked a volunteer at the convention. "Sid Haig."

Haig continued to have both a busy acting career and a great relationship with his fans up until his death. I've never heard a fan say anything bad about him. His performance as Captain Spaulding in Rob Zombie's movies was the cherry on a career already filled with memorable movie rolls. Haig even credited *House of 10,000 Corpses* with presenting him to a new generation of fans. For the last few years the Spaulding character has been as popular at Horror conventions as Freddy or Jason. I saw Haig appear at various conventions many times over the last decade. I'd just stand there and watch him interact with his fans. He publicly said that he tried to keep his convention prices to $20 for an item purchased from him, and $10 for a signature on something brought to him. No charge for a pic of you meeting him at his table. His pledge to keep prices down came at a time when B- and C-grade celebrities were charging up to $80 for a signed photo, and the conventions teamed up with companies to gouge fans for overpriced "professional photo ops." (Would you spend a few hundred dollars for a picture of you meeting all of the original Jasons, and you can't tell who they are because they have pillow cases over their heads? Fine, knock yourself out.)

There's a lot going to be written about Haig in this issue, so I won't close by trying to write a sappy obituary. A character may die in a movie, but you can always watch them again from the beginning. Movie performances stay alive as long as there are people who will watch them. Sid Haig wanted to entertain, always did his best, and he leaves a legacy behind in the Grindhouse that's available for us to see.

BLACK MAMA WHITE MAMA (1973) & SAVAGE SISTERS (1974)

By Louis Paul

One does not have to be an expert on trash cinema or exploitation movies to appreciate and enjoy the women in prison films of the sixties and seventies. If you weren't 'of age' during this period and able to see the heavy cream of exploitation movies in movie theaters, fear not, because many of these films, or at least the trailers for them, have been available throughout the years from a variety of sources, and companies. The movies have become available from sources as odd as no-name vendors who sold (more than likely unlicensed) film packages to Amazon Prime for streaming, to prestige companies like the UK-based Arrow who go all-out with their film restorations and extras.

The genre itself goes far back and can be traced to at least, a 1933 Pre-Code era title with Barbara Stanwyck called *Ladies They Talk About*, an Edgar Ulmer film from the 1940s called *Girls in Chains*, and the gritty and famously butch (for its time) *Caged* in 1950 was a turning point in not so thinly veiled girl-on-girl sadism and implied lesbianism. *Women's Prison* in 1955 with Ida Lupino and Jan Sterling, dialed the sadism back ever so slightly, but appeared to be the last, impressionable film in the genre for about ten years. Jess Franco, the Spanish filmmaker who dabbled in every genre imaginable partnered with Harry Alan Towers for 1969's *99*

Women. Although tame by comparison to many of Franco's later WIP films (most of them starring Lina Romay), this gritty, sadistic flick amped up the themes of the previously mentioned movies (more than likely, an influence on this one) and starred Maria Rohm as 'Marie', the 99th inmate on an island prison run by a paramilitary nutcase, and his sadistic lesbian warden cohort. Escape is on the menu here, followed by recapture, rape (sort of graphic for the time, but mainly implied) and a cast you wouldn't think you'd see in a film of this caliber—Bond girl Luciana Paluzzi, Rosalba Neri, Maria Schell, Mercedes McCambridge, and a real menacing turn by Herbert Lom.

When Roger Corman's New World Pictures production and distribution company started banging out exploitation films in the early seventies, a majority of the films moved production to the Philippines where the labor was cheaper, jungles available (a few hours from the main towns, cities and villages) and the acting pool (stunt persons, extras, smaller roles, and the occasional co-starring parts, Vic Diaz for example) was wide open. Jack Hill (director of *Spider Baby*, co-starring Sid Haig) filmed two of these sexy and sex-filled women in prison films. Each one more lurid that its predecessor. We had *The Big Doll House* (1971), and *The Big Bird Cage* (1972), both featured a prominent part for Sid Haig. A third film in this cycle, *Women in Cages* (1971) was directed by the Filipino director Gerardo De Leon (a co-producer on the *Blood* trilogy, he co-directed *Brides of Blood* and *Mad Doctor of Blood Island* with Eddie Romero [both 1968]), and it also walked a tightrope on the then emerging Blaxploitation genre by highlighting African American actresses Judith Brown and Juanita Collins.

American International Pictures then got into the game and decided to hire another Filipino filmmaker Eddie Romero (the *Blood* trilogy, *Beast of the Yellow Night* (1971), *The Twilight People* (1972), and others), and to film the movie in the Philippines. *Black Mama White Mama* (1973) starred Pam Grier and Margaret Markov (whom everyone thought was European, but she was from southern California). For the then suddenly popular Grier, this was like her sixth major role in a film in a three-year period. Markov, on the other hand, only did bit parts, some small TV appearances and besides this feature, juicy roles in *The Arena* (1974) (also with Pam), and the sleazy *The Hot Box* (1972). Sid Haig, who appeared in several Jack Hill's women in prison movies hams it up a bit, and nearly steals any scenes he appears in as a cowboy bounty hunter. Jonathan Demme's script veers away from some of the more lurid, creepy, downbeat elements that showed up in prior films in the genre and aims for a slightly lighter feel but still hits all the appropriate beats. Girls from opposite sides, check. Girls in shower scenes, check. Girls join forces and try to escape prison, check…and so on.

Because it's shot in the Philippines by primarily a Philippine production crew, much of the movie has this humid, nearly wet, lived-in look. The movie opens on a bus carrying women to a 'rehabilitation center'. Grier plays the tough black hooker, and Markov, a captured revolutionary fighter seeking to overthrow dictators in the (unnamed) country. Lynn Borden is the prison matron who wants to get 'close' to her female charges in ways that some of them may not take kindly to. "Strip 'em and get 'em wet' is one of her first orders to her minions as she eyes both our stars but more than likely decides Markov won't split her lip if she attempts to split her beaver with her tongue. In time, we learn that Grier's character may have been setup by her pimp, who just happens to be the island's biggest supplier of drugs.

Grier and Markov don't warm up so easily to each other, but after learning they will be transferred to a maximum-security facility in the city (if they ever get there alive) the duo form an alliance and plan an escape when Markov's guerilla fighters attack a transport vehicle. Through the jungles they go, and hot on their heels are a variety of casting agency types and Sid

Haig as a flamboyant cowboy bounty hunter. It's been said that the director, Eddie Romero allowed Sid to just run with the character and do whatever he wanted, essentially direct himself, and whether true or not, it certainly is one of Sid's more unusual early roles alternating between odd comic timing, and that sinister Sid we all know and love. No reason to note how all this ends, but you should check out the Arrow special edition Blu-ray. It truly looks terrific with some interesting extras.

*Carpi Asturias and Sid in **Black Mama White Mama**. Copyright American International Pictures.*

Eddie Romero returns as director for *Savage Sisters*, made the same year, but released in 1974. This one is a blender mix of every imaginable exploitation genre, and unfortunately, doesn't get much love and attention nowadays, and probably because the plot is all over the place. Former teen heartthrob and transplant to the Philippines (he was in all the *Blood* trilogy films for producer-director Romero) co-stars as an American conman from the south, who somehow gets involved with loot stolen from a criminal gang run by (Philippine national treasure) Vic Diaz and Sid Haig!

Bond girl Gloria Hendry (a year after a major role in *Live and Let Die*) plays a Policewoman named Lynn who teams up with Ashley and two revolutionaries (Cheri [*Ginger* flicks] Caffaro and [Filipino actress] Rosanna Ortiz as Mai Ling. No explanation is given for why the whiter than white, pale Caffaro has stayed so luminescent despite being jailed with Ortiz in a jungle jail run by sinister criminal Captain Morales and his horny soldiers. When Hendry learns that a million U.S. dollars (after all, this was the early seventies) was stolen by the revolutionaries, and in turn, by Morales and another criminal gang, the trio of women, sort of join up with Ashley to find the money. Hot on their trail, or tails, depending on how you look at it, are Vic Diaz and Sid Haig. I'm not sure if Romero gave Sid *carte blanche* to take his scripted lines and create another flamboyant, and odd character. It appears that Diaz and Sid were free to let go with their characters, creating odd comic villains with a sinister, and sleazy edge. Some of Sid's dialogue is priceless in this movie, sometimes nearly unintelligibly screaming asides or complaints to his goons when they prove themselves to be useless at being bad assess.

Add John Ashley's mustached lothario-cum-scammer-cum treasure hunter (or is he?), and a trio of ass-kicking babes, this one is about as much fun as watching a few Rudy Ray Moore movies back-to-back, meaning there's some charm, some camp, and a little bit of sleaze, but ultimately, it's not as entertaining as it could have been, and should have been. Surprisingly, top-billed Gloria Hendry, who is as tough as nails as Lynn, and Caffaro really don't ignite the screen. Sure, they're fine firing off weapons, and doing some sort of movie-fu martial arts, but Rosanna Ortiz comes off more sensual. Speaking of sensuality, for a later in the genre women in prison movie, there's very little of that, and with all the added action movie beats, and comedy breaks it all comes off as one schizo affair. Still, all in all these two films give us two rather unusual, and taken at face value, fun performances from the late Sid Haig.

SAVAGE SISTERS: SID GOES PSYCHO

1974's *Savage Sisters* seems to have been Sid's last film in the Philippines. This film was produced by AIP and its bigger budget shows. It was another John Ashley / Eddie Romero collaboration, but Ashley is a main character as hustler W.P. Billingsley. The film opens with W.P. telling us what's about to happen.

There is a briefcase with a million dollars en route to the general in charge of this tropical paradise. The rebels want it and have teamed up with psychotic bandit, Malavasi (Sid). Picture Eli Wallach's Tuco, from *The Good, the Bad, and the Ugly*, on crack, with a thick Mexican accent. His second-in-command is One Eye (Vic Diaz looking sleazier than usual because the clothes that he wears are too small for him). One of the rebels has a rich girlfriend, Jo Turner (Cheri Caffaro), who has joined the rebels. Mei Ling (Rosanna Ortiz) and her girls are supposed to blow up a bridge to start the robbery.

The combined forces wipe out the convoy. The two couriers are handcuffed to the briefcase. They are gunned down and Malavasi has their hands cut off. When they try and split the money, Malavasi turns on the rebels and his men kill them all. Malavasi kills his wounded men because wounded men slow you down.

Before the girls can act, they are surrounded by Captain Morales's men. They are cut down and only Jo and Mei survive. They are taken to Sgt. Lynn Jackson (Gloria Hendry) for interrogation. A dildo on a power drill is used on Jo. Then they are paraded by the press and set to be executed.

Malavasi had made a deal with W.P. to charter a plane to get him off the island. They meet at an airstrip where W.P. introduces Malavasi to WWII Ace Smilin' Jake (Bruno Punzalen). Jake wants five grand and pulls a gun when he sees the contents of the briefcase. Jake and Malavasi's men shoot it out, leaving all of Jake's men dead. Malavasi blames W.P. for the set up, but W.P. didn't know about the money. Malavasi decides to find a boat and goes to a black strip bar owner named Pegleg.

W.P., really pissed, goes to see Jackson and tells her about the million dollars. "We need those two girls to lead us to the cash," he tells her. Obviously they have some kind of sordid history. Jackson arranges a breakout and that becomes a bloody battle. Jo and Mei agree to help find the money for a four-way split. Jo doesn't care about the money, she want to kill Malavasi to avenger her lover.

Captain Morales (Eddie Garcia) is also hot on their trail, as he was promised a promotion to general if he succeeds. Malavasi is in a whore house with three girls that he kills before leaving. All parties converge on the docks to get Pegleg's boat. Morales brought troops and there

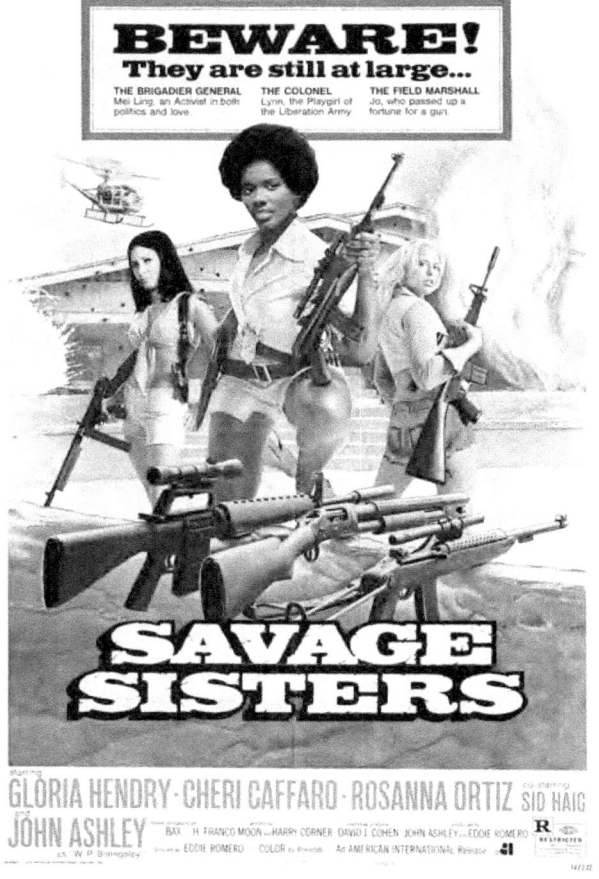

is a major battle. Pegleg gets blown up; Morales is run over by the girls in their jeep. W.P. tells Malavasi he want half the money to get him out. Malavas agrees, but turns on W.P., killing his man, Punjab.

Now W.P. joins forces with the girls. They corner Malavasi and One Eye. They bury the two up to their necks and the tide comes in and drowns them. W.P. tries to take the money, but his gun isn't loaded and the women beat his ass. Then they go their separate ways.

Sid is batshit crazy in this film as Malavasi. He channels his inner Mexican for this film. If you read his interview, you read that he was considered to do spaghetti westerns. Based on this performance, he would have been awesome. This film is a bit more violent than previous ones.

John Ashley produced and appeared in two more films, *Black Mamba* (1974) and *Sudden Death* (1977). He was an associate producer on *Apocalypse Now*. He became an executive producer for TV shows including *The A-Team, Werewolf, The Quest,* and others. His last on-screen appearance was a cameo in Fred Olen Ray's *Invisible Mom* in 1998. He was sitting in his car on location for *Scar City* in New York when he died from a massive heart attack at age 62.

I rewatched this film on a shaky DVD that I don't think is legit. This film needs a Blu Ray release. It's a grindhouse classic and one of Sid's best films.

THE HOST: HAIG & HILL, TOGETHER FOR THE FIRST TIME
By Robert Morgan

Sid Haig was just two months into his 80th full year of existence when he departed this mortal coil in September of last year, but he left behind one of the wildest and weirdest bodies of work an actor could possibly amass. Usually cast as the heavy, Haig alternated between film and television throughout his 60-year career in the entertainment industry and always brought his A-game to whatever role he was given—be it a lead, supporting character, or bit player.

Though his fan base knew him best from the countless low-budget horror films he featured in during the last years of his life, Haig's early days as an actor were the most fascinating. On the silver screen, he played a dapper Organization thug in John Boorman's classic Lee Marvin crime drama, *Point Blank*, a hulking brute in George Lucas's directorial debut *THX-1138*, and a hobo in Robert Aldrich's Depression-era adventure *Emperor of the North*. He also briefly appeared in *Diamonds Are Forever*, Sean Connery's comeback as James Bond. Prior to his death, Haig played a scavenger who meets a violent end in the opening scenes of S. Craig Zahler's exciting horror-western, *Bone Tomahawk*.

Outside of Rob Zombie, who gave him one of his career-defining roles in the form of the psychotic clown Captain Spaulding in *House of 1000 Corpses* and its grittier sequels *The Devil's Rejects* and *3 From Hell*, the director who employed Haig more than any other was Jack Hill. The two men worked together on eight feature films (including 1966's *Blood Bath*, which was a composite of scenes shot by Hill and Stephanie Rothman as well as footage from the obscure Yugoslavian thriller *Portrait of Terror*), but the project that first brought them together was an obscure short film Hill made when he was doing postgraduate studies at the UCLA Film School and Haig was studying the craft of acting at the renowned Pasadena Playhouse and rooming with Stuart Margolin.

The Host, running a lean half-hour, revolves around a cowboy, played by Haig, who has escaped from a Mexican jail and is seeking refuge from the authorities hot on his trail. He and his trusty horse come across a small village in the middle of nowhere that is sparsely populated.

The cowboy encounters a raven-haired beauty (Sharon Bercutt, an actress who had an uncredited bit part in the Elvis Presley western *Flaming Star* the same year she co-starred in Hill's short) who seems reluctant to speak to him at first. Then a maniac with wild hair and a look of murder in his eyes opens fire on the village's newest arrival. The cowboy is forced to take shelter with the lady, who explains to him the maddening situation he just moseyed on into.

The shooter is a Spaniard who came to the village a long time ago, and because his arrival was followed by a much-needed rainfall and a prosperous corn harvest, the villagers believed him to be a god. But then the rains dried up, the crops died, and the Spaniard descended into insanity. The woman now believes the cowboy to be his successor, but in order to take his place and ensure the village's survival, he must kill the Spaniard.

Under the woman's instruction, the cowboy rips a thick branch from a nearby tree, overcomes the Spaniard, and beats him to death with the branch. The rains finally return, and as the cowboy and woman make love in her house that night, the villagers make disturbing work of the Spaniard's corpse.

The next morning, our unlikely hero awakens from a good night's rest to find beautiful weather and his new lady friend bathing at a fountain. All seems to be well until he discovers the Spaniard's gruesome remains arranged in a ritualistic manner. Enough is enough. Satisfied that he killed the village's beastly overlord and brought the people renewed hope and prosperity, the cowboy prepares to leave.

The woman sets his horse free and it wanders away from the village before the cowboy realizes it. Unable to catch up to his once-loyal steed, he now understands the fate he has inherited. One day in the future, when the rains dry up once more and the health of the crops are threatened, it will be his turn to get taken out by the next poor sucker who happens upon the village. All he can do is be well-armed when that dark day comes (not that it would so much good though). The cowboy cries helplessly as his horse vanishes from sight, "I don't want to be a god!"

In addition to producing, editing, and directing *The Host*, Hill also wrote the screenplay for the short film after reading James Frazer's landmark 1890 study of religion and mythology, *The Golden Bough*. Frazer's writings have been hugely influential on celebrated authors such as James Joyce, William Butler Yeats, Camille Paglia, H.P. Lovecraft, and Ernest Hemingway. Jim Morrison even wrote a song for The Doors, "Not to Touch the Earth", inspired by *The Golden Bough*.

Watching *The Host*, anyone who has ever seen one of Hill's better-known features - be it his terrific racing drama *Pit Stop* or his classic Pam Grier duology *Coffy* and *Foxy Brown*—could see the future drive-in directing great sowing the seeds for his unique career in cinema. Hill effectively uses the simple set-up of a man on the run adrift in a village beset by evil to introduce several interesting philosophical concepts within the framework of a plot that could have made a fine episode of *The Virginian* or *Wanted: Dead or Alive*.

If you have only known Haig as the bald, bearded horror icon and avuncular convention celebrity beloved by fans all over the world, it might be jarring at first to see the actor as he was starting out. Lanky, clean-shaven, and with a full head of hair, he makes for a convincing cowpoke with a troubling past. Cool and charming, Haig also confronts the story's weightier intellectual themes without becoming overwhelmed by them. Hill could not have asked for a better leading man for *The Host*, and the short serves as perfect evidence that the director and his star would work beautifully together in the years to come.

In its absence from circulation, the cultural legacy of *The Host* grew thanks the similarities between its plot and the third act of Francis Ford Coppola's hallucinatory Vietnam War masterpiece *Apocalypse Now*. Hill and Coppola had been friends and classmates at UCLA, and Hill had worked as a cinematographer and editor on Coppola's early sex comedies *Tonight for Sure* and *The Bellboy and the Playgirls*.

Stephen Burum, who served as cinematographer on *The Host*, went on to work as a second unit cameraman on *Apocalypse Now*. He later reported to Hill that Coppola, unsatisfied with the

Copyright Rolling Thunder Pictures.

ending of John Milius's script, decided to fashion an ending loosely inspired by Hill's student short. The director even went as far as to include a copy of *The Golden Bough* among the private library of Marlon Brando's Colonel Kurtz.

Apocalypse Now was infamously filmed in the Philippines during its rainy season, when destructive hurricanes reduced its expensive sets to rubble and kindling. Hill had earlier made the women-in-prison classics *The Big Bird Cage* and *The Big Doll House* (both starring Grier, with Haig in supporting roles) in the same country for Roger Corman's New World Pictures. It was Corman who had cautioned Coppola against shooting *Apocalypse* in the Philippines when the inclement weather would be at its worst, but the arrogant filmmaker obviously didn't heed the B-movie legend's warning. Hill would also have given Coppola the same advice had he been consulted.

Burum later reteamed with Coppola, this time as the cinematographer, for the filmmaker's S.E. Hinton adaptations, *The Outsiders* and *Rumble Fish*, and became Brian DePalma's go-to man behind the camera on nearly every film he made from *Body Double* to *Mission to Mars*. Hill's assistant director on *The Host* was the Egypt-born Farouk "Frank" Agrama. Best known to cult movie fans for exploitation flicks like *Queen Kong* and *Dawn of the Mummy*, Agrama found his greatest career success as one of the producers of the blockbuster miniseries *Shaka Zulu* and the founder and CEO of the production company Harmony Gold USA, which brought the popular Japanese animated franchise *Robotech* to American audiences.

Donald Shebib, the designer of a miniature version of the village set used in some shots, later became a prominent film and television director in his native Canada. The role of production supervisor was fulfilled by Dorothy Arzner, Hill's instructor at the UCLA Film School and Haig's acting teacher at the Pasadena Playhouse. From 1927-1943, Arzner made three silent films and fourteen sound films as the only female director working in the Golden Age of Hollywood.

The Host didn't receive a home video release until it was included as a bonus feature on the first DVD of Hill's girl gang action classic *Switchblade Sisters*. Arrow Video also presented the short as an extra on their Blu-ray release of *Spider Baby*, the first film Hill made with Haig (shot in 1964, though not released theatrically until 1967). I highly recommend you seek out either video edition so you can watch *The Host* and watch as two legendary careers in film are born before your very eyes.

"I LIVE, AND I DIE, BY THE CRYSTALS!"
The Unsung Classic, *Galaxy of Terror*

By Terrence Cain

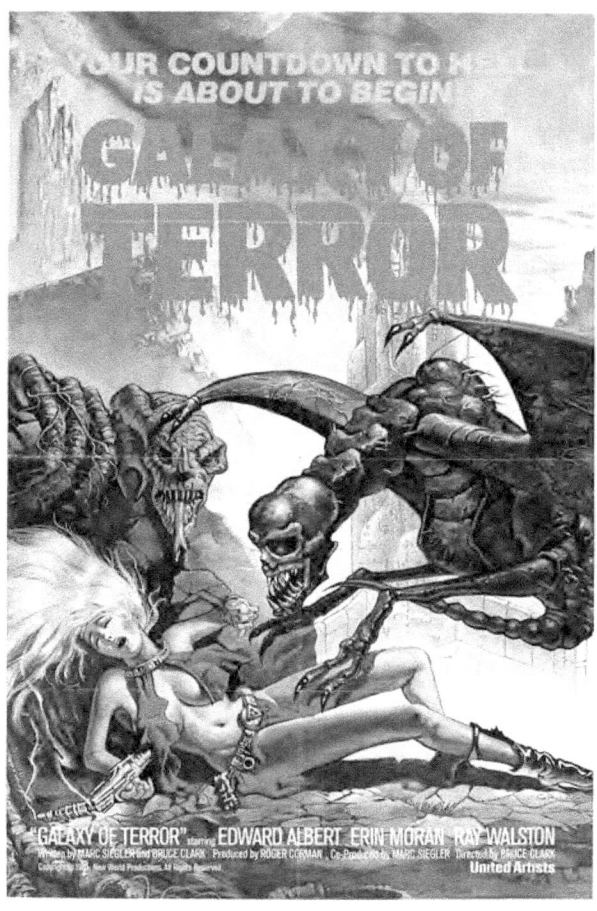

At around the 35:10 mark we see Zalman King [Baelon] approach Sid Haig [Quuhod] who has a look of disgust, most likely for the director, before delivering his only line: "I live, and I die, by the crystals!" Then Haig's eyes slightly bulge. At that very moment you can clearly tell Haig threw up a little in his mouth.

Released in October 1981, *Galaxy of Terror* would be another knock-off from New World Pictures. Inspired by Ridley Scott's 1979 masterpiece, *Alien*, *Galaxy of Terror* wouldn't have the cultural impact of its inspiration, but nonetheless it's a great film. It even managed to become a mild success as the movie made $4 million against its $1.3 million budget. Much of the film's success is due in part to future director James Cameron, famous for such films as *The Terminator*' *Aliens*, and *The Abyss*, who was able to make the special effects look like they cost much more.

In 1980, producer Roger Corman approached director Bruce D. Clark, and screenwriter Marc Siegler. After their initial meeting with Corman, Siegler decided to write a script about a group of outer space travelers who go to another planet where they confront their worst fears.

Originally titled *Planet of Horrors*, Corman was having trouble casting. Upon production assistant David DeCoteau's recommendation the script was temporarily renamed *Quest* after

*The Cast of **Galaxy of Terror**. All Photos copyright New World Pictures. All Rights Reserved.*

the main spaceship.

During early promotion the film was titled *Mind Warp: An Infinity of Terror*. That title didn't go so well, and since Corman didn't think the original title was grandiose enough, *Galaxy of Terror* was the final title.

According to Haig, Corman approached him for the role of Quuhod. Upon reading the script Haig loved it and wanted to play the role with one stipulation. Haig wanted to play Quuhod as a mute. The reason behind it, Haig has said, was that he felt the dialogue written did not match the personality of the character. Corman agreed, but Clark did not, and thus one line of dialogue made its way into Haig's mouth.

According to Robert Englund, who played Ranger, Haig helped guide some of the greener actors who were feeling anxious during the making of the film. Englund seemed to be very appreciative of Haig upon his retelling of events during the making of the movie, available on the DVD special, *Roger Corman's Cult Classics: Galaxy of Terror*, released by Shout! Factory.

While *Galaxy of Terror* is not a perfect film by any stretch of the imagination, particularly because of the bad dialogue and acting of Grace Zabriskie, who played Captain Trantor, not to mention the bizarreness of Ray Walston's character [Kore] being a pseudo-Yoda and Darth Vader all rolled into one, I personally enjoy this movie because of the great acting chops of Englund and Haig, and Cameron's special effects as well. Englund's performance during his bout with his doppelganger is amazing. This scene alone gives the audience an insight to what would make Englund so great when he became Freddy Krueger in the franchise *A Nightmare On Elm Street*. Haig's performance is equally fantastic, and most definitely the best part of the film. Haig is able to emote so much with facial expressions and hand gestures. From this one performance alone I feel Haig would've been a superstar actor in the silent era, perhaps even giving Lon Chaney, Sr. a run for his money.

I've loved Haig's work since I first saw this film on VHS back in 1990 thanks to a friend whose stepfather owned a copy. I was probably far too young to see it, seeing how I was seven at the time, but I'm forever grateful I was introduced to Haig at such a young age. May Haig's essence live on in the hearts and minds of his fans. You will be missed, but most certainly not forgotten.

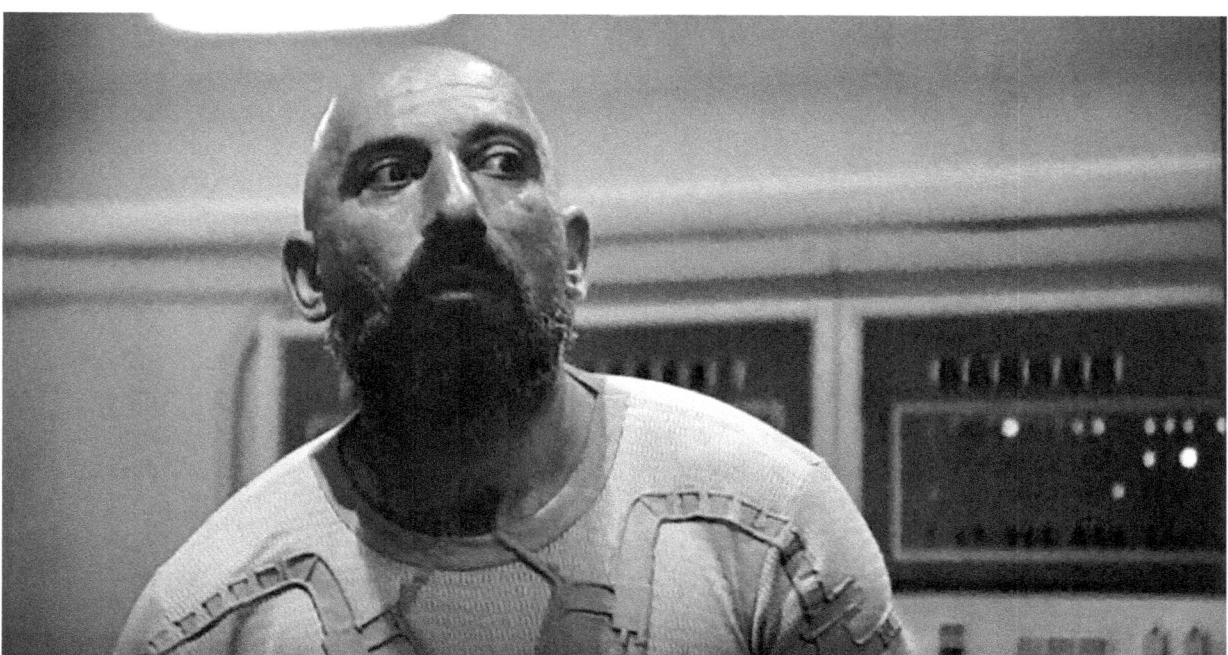

SID, PAM AND JACK: FUN IN THE PHILIPPINES
by Bill Adcock

All photos this section copyright New World Pictures. All Rights Reserved.

In 1970, Roger Corman left American International Pictures and founded New World Pictures, intending to continue to crank out low-budget exploitation movies that could be distributed globally. With some early successes in the form of Angels Die Hard and The Student Nurses, New World Pictures was off to a great start, and then, a script called "The Big Doll House" crossed Corman's desk. Women in Prison films were nothing new, but the film's setting—a women's prison in a tropical banana republic—was promising. A conversation with John Ashley (along with a check to help cover production) convinced Corman to shoot it in the Philippines. Corman handed it off to Jack Hill to direct, Jack Hill hired his frequent collaborator Sid Haig, as well as bombshell newcomer Pam Grier, to act in the film.

That's where gold was struck, but I'm getting ahead of myself.

The Big Doll House follows some of the pre-established tropes of the "Women in Prison" genre—women railroaded into unfair convictions, sadistic lesbian guards, and the climactic prison break. However, it breaks from tradition by refusing to focus on one woman for the duration of the film; instead, like The Student Nurses, its an ensemble film following the stories of multiple women leading up to the climax. It's a solid entry in the WIP genre, and turned a tidy enough profit that Corman was quickly champing at the bit to shoot more movies in the Philippines.

The director-actor combination of Jack Hill and Sid Haig, going back to *Spider Baby*, is a potent one, with both men playing off each other's strengths. Adding Pam Grier, with her statuesque beauty and magnetic personality, was pouring gasoline onto dynamite. As top bitch "Grear" in the film, Grier snarled and sneered her way through her scenes, proving a more memorable villain than the warden and her goons. Jack Hill would go on to direct her (and Sid) in *Coffy, Foxy Brown*, and of course, *The Big Bird Cage*.

When asked to direct a sequel to *The Big Doll House*, Jack Hill was left scratching his head. What else was there for him to say about women's prisons? So he decided to crank the absurdity up and make *The Big Bird Cage* as much a parody of the WIP genre as it was a part of it.

This time around, Haig has a much larger role as the guerrilla fighter Django, with Grier as his submachine-gun-toting girlfriend, Blossom. After a successful robbery to fund their operations, the two come to the conclusion that recruitment rates for their revolutionary army would skyrocket if they had some hot and horny women to offer new recruits as incentive. To that end, Blossom agrees to go undercover as an inmate at the local women's prison—a hellish place where women are forced to labor barefoot on the titular Bird Cage, a huge bamboo contraption (grinding grain into flour, I think) under the watchful eyes and rifles of sneering gay male guards (subverting the lesbian guard trope common in WIP films). Once Blossom has riled the girls up, Django disguises himself as flamboyant hairdresser "Tham Thmith" and seduces his way past the guards to start the prison break in earnest.

For those of you used to seeing Sid Haig play a hulking villain, seeing him lean and young with a wax-styled mustache, lispingly flirting with professional leering sweaty fat guy Vic Diaz, is something unimaginable, but it just goes to show what a talent Haig was. It's an odd film, in that everything is played for laughs, including the vicious gang rape of the male guards by the inmates at the film's climax. I'm not sure how audiences at the time reacted to this much wacky comedy in their grimy, borderline pornographic women-in-prison films, but it's a surreal thing to see today.

The Big Doll House and *The Big Bird Cage* are two of the foundational films of New World Pictures, Roger Corman's successor to AIP, and without the trio of Jack Hill, Sid Haig and Pam Grier, I can't see how they'd have been the successes they were and the iconic films they continue to be today, especially *The Big Bird Cage*.

SID HAIG: IMPOSSIBLE MISSIONS HEAVY
By Ken Brunette

*Sid in one of his appearances in **Mission: Impossible.***
(All photos this section copyright Paramount Television. All Rights Reserved.)

Sid Haig appeared as various henchmen and heavies on the hit TV series *Mission: Impossible* in a total of nine episodes between 1966-1970. An innovative series inspired partly by the heist film *Topkapi* (1964), it was created by Bruce Geller during the spy craze of the 1960's. It starred Steven Hill (*Raw Deal*) as Impossible Missions Force (IMF) leader Dan Briggs, Martin Landau (*Without Warning*) as master-of-disguise Rollin Hand, Landau's off-screen wife Barbara Bain (*Don't Go Near the Park*) as fashion model Cinnamon Carter, Greg Morris (*Cool Red*) as electronics expert Barney Collier, and Peter Lupus (*Hercules and the Tyrants of Babylon*) as strongman Willy Armitage.

Fakeout (1966). This first season episode guest-starred Lloyd Bridges (*Airplane!*) as an international drug dealer. It features one of the infrequent occurrences of the IMF team knocking back a few. Sid meets a gruesome end when he is thrown into a polar bear den during a fight with Barney.

The Slave (1967) Parts 1 & 2. The second season saw a major change as Hill was replaced with Peter Graves (*Stalag 17*) as new IMF leader Jim Phelps after disagreements between Hill and the shows producers. With a no-nonsense demeanor and solid background in B-movies, Graves was the perfect replacement. *The Slave* was one of several two-parters, with this plot concerning the bust-up of a Muslim slave ring. Guest stars include Warren Stevens (*Forbidden Planet*) and Antoinette Bower (*Prom Night*). A grudge develops between Sid and Phelps, which is resolved in Part 2 by Sid ending up on the wrong end of a gun.

Trial by Fury (1968). The IMF infiltrates a prison camp in a totalitarian South American country in order to save an innocent man. Viewers may recognize the prison set as Stalag 13 from *Hogan's Heroes*. Guest stars include Michael Tolan (*All That Jazz*), Victor French (*Rio Lobo*), and Paul Winfield (*Star Trek II: The Wrath of Khan*). Sid has a solid role in this as one of the head prisoners and we catch glimpses of the wild laugh he was known for in exploitation films.

The Diplomat (1968). Despite behind-the-scenes upheaval involving the producers and writers, season three was the critical and creative high point of the series. Guest-starring Fernando Lamas (*The Cheap Detective*) as enemy diplomat Roger Toland. The beautiful Lee Grant (*In the Heat of the Night*) as IMF agent Susan Buchanan, is featured in a harrowing race-against-time sequence where she is drugged and has 15 minutes to live. Sid plays Grigor, an enemy agent in possession of vital U.S. defense secrets.

Doomsday (1969). The IMF must stop a European industrialist (Alf Kjellin, *Ice Station Zebra*) from selling a hydrogen bomb to the highest bidder and keep it out of the hands of third-world powers. Sid plays Marko, bodyguard to arms purchaser Kura (Arthur Batanides, *Brannigan*).

Commandante (1969). Season 4 saw another major shift with Martin Landau and Barbara Bain leaving the series over salary disputes. Leonard Nimoy, fresh off the cancellation of *Star Trek*, was brought in as master-of-disguise Paris. The IMF goes undercover in a Latin American country in order to save an imprisoned priest from execution. Sid has his biggest role and possibly definitive performance of the series as the revolutionary Major Carlos Martillo. Also guest-starring Lawrence Dane (*Scanners*).

The Choice (1970). The IMF must stop a self-proclaimed mystic from using his influence over the Grand Duchess of Trent (Nan Martin, *Jackson County Jail*) to take over political control. Also guest-starring Arthur Franz (*Monster on the Campus*). Sid plays a palace guard who ends up on the wrong end of a silencer.

Decoy (1970). The fifth season introduced Lesley Warren as IMF Agent Dana Lambert and a young Sam Elliott as Dr. Doug Robert in an effort to boost ratings and appeal to a youth audience. It also featured a funkier rendition of Lalo Schifrin's iconic main title theme. The IMF aids a communist dictators' daughter (Julie Gregg, *The Godfather*) in defecting to the U.S. with a list of American agents. Michael Strong (*Point Blank, Patton*), and Paul Stevens (*Battle for the Planet of the Apes*) guest star. Sid makes his last appearance of the series as Agent #1. The final two seasons saw a move away from international espionage and more to organized crime.

Sid's menacing stare, imposing frame, and sinister laugh made him a character actor like no other and perfect for the demands of the series.

SID HAIG IN BUSTING (1974)

by John Rieber

The 1974 film *Busting* stars Elliot Gould and Robert Blake as Los Angeles police detectives who, naturally, play by their own rules. They stumble upon a local mobster, Rizzo, played by Alan Garfield, and ultimately embark on a game of cat-and-mouse as they try to bust him.

Busting has been referenced as the main inspiration for the *Starsky & Hutch* TV series.

Sid Haig has a small but pivotal role as Rizzo's main bodyguard. *Busting* was one of three films Haig appeared in along with four TV shows in 1974. Sid was always working!

Haig shows up almost an hour into the film, as the two cops begin to harass the mobster. When they go into one of Rizzo's strip clubs, Sid comes over to talk to them. He is dressed very nicely, with a sharp suit and goatee, exuding a menacing sophistication. He doesn't confront the cops as much as engage them in a conversation, politely reminding them that they aren't allow in the club, suggesting his boss pays the cops off to leave him alone.

That prompts the duo to go renegade, and they begin stalking Rizzo on their own time.

When Rizzo fakes a heart attack, they stake out the hospital.

At one point they barge into Rizzo's hospital room where Haig is guarding him. A nurse arrives to chastise the cops, "You can't be here," she barks to them, "only immediately family!"

"Oh yeah? Well he's no immediate family," Gould says, pointing to Haig. "He's a creep!" After they are tossed out, the cops realize that Rizzo is getting far too many flowers going in and out of

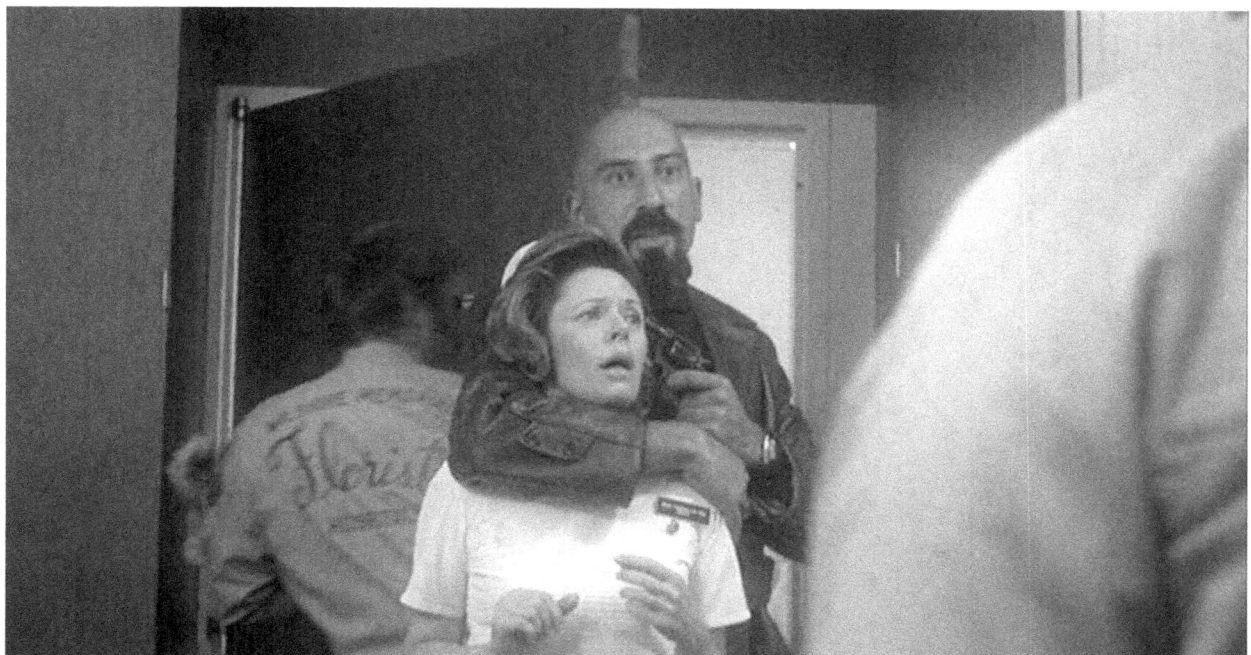

Photo Copyright United Artists. All Rights Reserved.

his room, and realize that drugs are being smuggled through the hospital. This leads to Haig's terrific action sequence, as he takes a nurse hostage, steals an ambulance, and leads the cops on a great chase through the Los Angeles streets.

Sid manages to drive the ambulance at a high speed AND turn to fire at the cops. Ultimately, he crashes and is shot in the back while trying to escape.

(Stunt coordinator on the film was Hal Needham, who went on to direct *The Cannonball Run* as well as many other films.)

Haig's role is small, but central to most of the scenes with Rizzo. He is always hovering, there to protect his boss. His gravitas on screen lends a smart, menacing quality to the film. Sid said in an interview that when he arrived on set they had been shooting for a couple of days. He said that he did his lines and someone started talking. Sid thought that maybe he didn't get all the pages or that they changed the script. They told him that they tossed the script out weeks ago. So the dialog in *Busting* was 90% improvised.

THE BLU-RAY REPORT: BEYOND ATLANTIS
by John Shatzer

*The cast of **Beyond Atlantis**.*
Photos copyright Dimension Pictures. All Rights Reserved.

When Pete had mentioned wanting to do a tribute issue to the late Sid Haig, I immediately started thinking about how I could tie him into my usual article here at Grindhouse Purgatory. He appeared in so many great movies over the years that I was sure there was one with a recent Blu-Ray release that I could cover. After a few minutes it hit me that I had the new release of the drive-in classic *Beyond Atlantis* from the fine folks at VCI sitting in my to watch pile. A movie that I've always been a huge fan of. This might be the easiest decision I've had to make when it comes to what to cover.

In case you haven't seen this movie, I'll give you a brief recap of the plot. Things kick off with a fisherman, portrayed by Filipino legend Vic Diaz, dropping off some supplies to a beautiful blonde woman. She pays for them with pearls and the man leaves. As soon as he is out of sight some strange fish eyed natives come from the woods and she gives them orders while disrobing. Okay movie you have my attention.

The action then moves to the city where the same fisherman is selling the pearls to East Eddie, played by Haig. Immediately realizing the value and rarity of the pearls, he attempts to pump the man for information, but the fisherman gives nothing but where he lives. This he will regret later. Later Eddie recruits a couple other Americans, Vic and Logan, to help him locate the source of the pearls. Together they make plans for their expedition and along the way are forced to bring along a woman named Kathy. She overheard them talking and as a scientist trying to make her mark realizes the pearls they have look much like some from an ancient stone mask she has been studying. Making some connections she threatens her own expedition including getting the authorities involved if she can't join theirs. Along with some of Eddie's men and the crew from Vic's boat they head off.

After a quick stop at the fisherman's village, where they rough him up for the location of the mysterious island, they arrive at their destination. They find some abandoned huts, but eventually do meet up with the natives. You have the odd-looking locals, those fish eyed natives mentioned earlier, as well as the beautiful woman and her father. We find out her name is Syrene and her father is Nereus. I'm jumping ahead a bit here but since it is in the title it should come as no surprise that they are descendants of refugees from the lost city of Atlantis. The timing of their arrival couldn't be better since it is time for Syrene to mate with an outsider. Once that is accomplished then they can be committed to the sea, which is a nice way of saying they are going to murder the hell out of them! Some shenanigans go down with rejection, jealousy, greed, and a couple other sins before we get the explosive and somewhat odd ending.

Let me chat about my personal connection with *Beyond Atlantis* before I get into the general discussion of the qualities of the movie. I've mentioned more than once in these pages that I grew up with a lot of these films. This isn't one of them. My first exposure to *Beyond Atlantis* was at Cinema Wasteland, a convention that I'm sure many of you readers are familiar with. They were showing the movie on 16mm film one Saturday night and I plopped down to watch it and was sucked right in. The next morning, I went looking in the dealer's room for a copy of the movie to take home with me. The only thing available at the time was a bootleg that I think was sourced from another 16mm print. I can say that because I went right home and watched it again noticing different defects from what I had seen the night before. For years this was the best version that I could find, but I'll save that discussion for later.

Now to the movie itself. The plot is tight and quickly introduces our characters before setting them off towards the island. It doesn't feel rushed at all, but you still get a good idea who Vic, East Eddie, and Logan are in just a couple scenes. This includes some killer dialogue from Haig's Eddie that lets you know where he is coming from right away. The line to one of his working girls, "You go pop for papa" sums his character up nicely. Toss in a fun bit of dialogue at the bar with Logan and Vic to cement who is playing what role in the rest of the story. For the most part the pacing of the story is perfect. Though as much as I love *Beyond Atlantis*, I will admit that some of the underwater scenes do drag, but the stuff surrounding them more than makes up for it. No matter how many times I watch it I'm never bored.

The cast for the movie is very impressive and includes John Ashley who was a frequent collaborator with director Eddie Romero and helped produce many of his movies in the seventies. I thought it was fun to see Ashely get a chance to play a heel here as he was normally cast as the romantic lead/hero. His character Logan is a greedy, womanizing, compulsive gambler that is always looking for an angle to score big. Patrick Wayne, yes John Wayne's son is in this, plays the stoic good guy Vic. This role reminded me of a lot of his father's western characters as he is fairly quiet. Wayne is decent but honestly is by far the least interesting of our leads. Vic Diaz has a very small part in the movie, but it is memorable. The guy is a legend in Filipino entertainment and pops up in a lot of the productions made for the U.S. market.

Finally, we come to Sid Haig's performance. The guy was awesome in just about everything that he appeared in so there were a lot of movies to choose from. As much as I enjoy his collaborations with Jack Hill and his renaissance as Captain Spaulding later on, this is my favorite performance/movie from his legendary career. From the moment he is on screen, Haig owns every scene he appears in. Not only is he physically imposing, but his quick dialogue delivery blows everyone else away. I have a feeling that director Eddie Romero knew this as he basically gives him all the best lines. This is the movie that made me appreciate who Haig was as a performer and in my humble opinion also laid the groundwork for what was to come. I think that East Eddie has more than a little bit of Captain Spaulding in him.

Since I'm reviewing the Blu-Ray release and not just the movie I suppose I should talk about the special features. This is easy because there isn't much offered on this release from VCI. You do get a fifteen-minute-long short titled *Remembering John Ashley* which I was very interested in. The guy did a lot of work and not much is out there on his career but sadly this didn't meet my expectations. If you have seen the excellent *Machete Maidens* documentary, then you will recognize most of this material as being recycled from it. There are interviews with Sid Haig, Patrick Wayne, and Eddie Romero to name just a few. But sadly, they couldn't even give Ashley his fifteen minutes as halfway thru it becomes all about working with Eddie Romero. I was bummed by this. The rest of the features are the typical inclusion of television spots, theatrical trailer, and photo gallery. Not much to it at all. Though I've saved the best for last.

Until this Blu-Ray the only copies I could ever find were from 16mm prints or, even worse, the occasional dreadful VHS rip. Finally, I was watching a digital transfer from a 35mm negative, and oh my God it was like watching the movie for the first time. The picture and sound are amazing and genuinely blew me away. I've revisited it twice in the week since my first viewing and I still shocked by how good it is.

I'm dangerously close to totally nerding out here so I'll stop. Clearly, I love *Beyond Atlantis* and this release made me very happy. For many years I've been telling anyone who would listen that this was my favorite drive-in movie. It also has one of Sid Haig's best performances and just got a beautiful new release. Does it get any better than this? I don't think so and highly recommend that anyone reading this go out and get themselves a copy.

This brings things to a close. As always you can email me at gutmunchers@gmail.com with any questions or comments on this latest installment of the Blu-Ray Report. Agree or disagree I'd love to hear from you. Though if you disagree on this one you had better bring your "A" game cause I'm ready! I'll see you all again here on the pages of this fine publication in six months to either steer you towards or away from the latest release. And as always, I can't thank 42nd Street Pete enough for the chance to participate in such a great project.

SID BY THE SEA
Mike Haushalter

There was a time in the early seventies where it seemed like every B movie made in the Philippines featured Sid Haig in it at some point. This is an exaggeration to be sure (before you send my editor an angry letter pointing out I am wrong), but he is in 7 of them. Over the years I have watched them all numerous times but if you wanted me to pick my favorites I would have to go with *Beyond Atlantis* and *The Wonder Women*.

Beyond Atlantis (1973)

A trio of racketeering fortune-hunters search for a reported fortune in undersea pearls somewhere to the south of the Philippines and discover not only the treasure but a tribe of merpeople who may be descendants of the lost continent of Atlantis.

Beyond Atlantis is an Eddie Romero-helmed pulp adventure that feels like a kind of south seas *Treasure of the Sierra Madre* crossed with a jungle flick. It has a decent script, some beautiful underwater photography, a fantastic soundtrack and a great cast including Patrick Wayne, John Ashley, Sid Haig, George Nader and Vic Diaz . For my money *Beyond Atlantis* is one of Sid's best roles of the time period (and maybe one of his biggest of the era). HIs character, East Eddie, a blustery cigar chomping pirate is one of the heroes for a change and the part is a good showcase for his roguish charm and personality, I also love that his characters greatest aspiration for the treasure they hope to find is four walling his family of prostitutes. Patrick Wayne and John Ashley (sporting some of the loudest shirts you have ever seen) are equally good as East Eddie's partners Vic Mathias and Logan. Vic (Wayne) is the square-jawed hero of the bunch (or at least the close to one as this film gets) a daredevil scuba diver and boat captain trying to get his partners to leave while the getting is good. Logan (Ashley) is the greedy bastard of the three (there's Daffy Duck and then him) and he could very well be a continuation of the surfer character he played in all those Frankie and Annete beach films all grown up and suffering from alcohol abuse and PTSD after a few tours of duty in Vietnam. George Nader (Jerry Cotton) is also of note as Nereus, the last king of Atlantis. He sports a beard straight out of *Hercules Unchained* and looks every inch like a peplum Greek god.

Would've, could've, should've, *Beyond Atlantis* is one of those films that really just missed out on being a cult favorite. Sadly, however, its producers thought they could make a family adventure that would appeal to a bigger audience and demanded that the film be PG-rated instead of the R-rated drive-in fare coming in from the Philippines. Maybe if it had an underwater monster, some swashbuckling sword fights, or just a few solid *mano a mano* punch-ups it could have been the film the moneymen were hoping for. Instead they got something that feels a bit like an edited for television version of an over ripe drive in outing.

I am not saying I don't like the film, quite the contrary I am fond of it, watched it a number of times and even picked up a copy on Blu-Ray. I just feel like it could have been a more memorable and exciting movie if John Ashley's original vision of an undersea race of topless mermaids would have been utilized and the action scenes punched up with more blood and thunder.

Wonder Women (1973)

Ex-CIA agent turned-Lloyd's of London's insurance investigator, Mike Harber (Ross Hagen), clashes with the depraved Dr. Tsu (Nancy Kwan) and her army of female assassins as he searches Manila for a missing jai-alai player with a million dollar policy.

Wonder Women is a fast paced and exciting b movie vanity project for rugged tough guy Ross Hagen (who also has a production credit on the film). It's an ahead of its time story of a black market organ harvesting/trafficking outfit run by the Dr. No-like Dr. Tsu (Nancy Kwan) and her sisterhood of assassins. It's loaded with crazy high-speed car chases, shoot outs, cock fighting, freaks of nature and kung fu fighting that would make Dolomite proud.

Much like *Beyond Atlantis*, *Wonder Women* offered a great role for Sid Haig and ample screen time to show off his acting chops. Here he plays Dr. Tsu's right hand man and majordomo Gregorious, a sharp dressed, debonair moneyman complete with frilly shirts and a sword cane a kind of slick old school mob mouthpiece that is far removed from most of his other roles that came out of the Philippines.

Ross Hagen also has a great part as cocksure egotistical insurance investigator Mike Harbor, a sexist, misogynist dinosaur who makes Sean Connery seem woke. He may not be the every woman wants to bed him, every man wants to be him hero that Bond is but I have seen worse (much worse), Of course in today's world he would probably be spending most of his time in meetings about sexual harassment with human resources instead of in the field.

WONDER WOMEN: SID'S FOURTH FILIPINO FILM

Wonder Women was not a Corman film. It was produced by its main star, Ross Hagen. How Sid got involved was by chance. He and Pam Grier were having breakfast when Hagen and director, Robert O'Neil spotted them. Taken by Sid's looks, they wrote the part of Gregorious, the evil lawyer, for him. Sid said he was ready to go home, but they got him.

This film is more over-the-top than previous films shot in the Philippines. In addition to Sid, Filipino regulars Vic Diaz and Bruno Punzalan were also cast. Plus Roberta Collins. Vic is Lapu Lapu , the cab driver. Bruno is a fisherman. Roberta is Laura, one of the assassins. Nancy Kwan is Dr. Tsu. Maria De Aragon is Linda, another assassin. Hagen is Mike Harber, ex CIA agent turned insurance investigator.

The film opens with some women drugging and kidnapping star athletes. We are treated to a few clumsy Kung Fu fights. Dr. Tsu is doing bargain basement transplants on her private island. She created the ultimate anti rejection drug that allows her to transplant any organ into any body. She sells body parts to dying millionaires. She has a billionaire, Mr. Paulson, on tap as he needs a new body. Her ladies grab a world class lacross player for this purpose.

Harber is hired to find these athletes. The insurance company stands to lose millions if they have to pay out death benefits. They want the athletes found quickly. Harber negotiates a deal that will make him 160 thousand dollars if he succeeds. He enlists the aid of cabbie, Lapu Lapu.

Lapu has a really cool cab. But word has gotten out and Dr. Su is told by her lawyer, Gregorious, that he has to be dealt with. Gregorious is negotiating with Paulson's people for a huge payday.

Lapu takes Haber to meet Nono, a fisherman. This scene takes place during a cockfight. It seems a couple of Nano's friends were fishing near a certain island and were never seen again. Nano also netted some human bones while fishing. Harber wants Nano to take them to the island. Nano refuses. Some young kid is watching all this. When Harber says, "Let's discuss this outside." They see Nano is now dead with a spike in his neck. The kid took him out.

A hit squad is sent after Harber, Lapu's cab is attacked, but Harber bails. Harber has a shotgun pistol that he blasts his attackers with. He gets away and Lapu asks who he pissed off. Back on the island, Tsu's minions have "brain sex." It is a device that wraps around your head and gives you mind-blowing orgasms. Today we call that the Internet. Linda, however, wants the real thing.

She is sent to kill Harber, but screws him before trying to kill him. Another clumsy bout of Kung Fu as Linda and Hagen pummel each other. Linda escapes and hijacks a cab, Haber and Lapu are in hot pursuit. This is a crazy chase though the streets of Manila. It took three days to shoot and there was no crowd control. The scene of a guy getting hit by the cab was unplanned. The guy was a drunk security guard who wandered into the scene. He was just banged up a bit.

The chase is really off the hook and you wonder how no one else got hurt. Linda's cab winds up in the water. Haber and Lapu make her take them to the island. Linda escapes, but is on Dr. Tsu's shitlist. She begs for another chance to capture Harber. Linda leads a group of heavily armed women to get Harber. After a shoot out, Haber is captured. He is brought to Dr. Tsu who is having dinner with Gregorious.

Haber insults Gregorious and the two have words. Harber is given a tour after Tsu and Gregorious talk about how much his body might be worth. Haber is shown where Tsu keeps her "mistakes", a bunch of jail cells with victims of her "surgeries " that are now psychotic killers. She shows him her organ bank and he sees the guy he is supposed to rescue being kept in a comatose state.

Tsu tries the brain sex on Haber that leaves him semiconscious. She has Linda arrested and tells her that for her failures, she will be dissected. Linda is taken away by Laura (Roberta Collins), who really doesn't like her. Tsu is now doing her brain transplant on Mr Paulsen. Linda and Laura fight Kung Fu style. Laura loses. Another girl, fed up with Tsu, helps Linda. She frees the mistakes who go on a killing rampage. Gregorious hears the alarm and wisely decides to leave.

He runs into the mistakes killing people. One guy grabs Linda but Gregoriuos dispatches him with his sword cane. Paulson dies on the operating table. Tsu dismisses her assistants. When Harber finds the athlete he was paid to save, Tsu taunts him that she will return. Harber collects his reward, but knows that Tsu will be after him. The film ends with Tsu's women going after Haber.

Wonder Women is a wild ride. Sid plays Gregorious pretty straight, as he is a deal maker and not a henchman. When we first see him, he is wearing a suit. By the end of the film, he seems to be wearing a purple pantsuit with a white tuxedo shirt. Maria De Aragon was the only actress that had to be flown in. Everyone else was already working there. Maria was only in twelve films. She was in *Nightmare in the Sun* (1965), *Bloodmania* (1970) and *The Cremators* (1973). Her last film was *Street Wars* in 1991.

Ross Hagen was a busy character actor who was in biker films like *The Hellcats, The Mini Skirt Mob*, both 1968, and *Five the Hard Way* (1969). He was also in *Avenging Angel* (1985) and *Armed Response* (1986). He was in twenty films for director Fred Olen Ray. He was a producer and director, producing ten films and directing eight of them. He died at age 72 in 2011.

Roberta Collins was a staple of the women-in-prison genre. Her last film was *Vendetta* in 1986, where she played against type as Warden Dice. Sadly she fell into the trap of drugs and alcohol and died from an overdose at age 63. She was married to Paul Harper, who played one of the bounty hunters in *The Wild Bunch*. Director Robert O'Neil also directed *Angel* (1984) and *Avenging Angel* (1985), plus *The Psycho Lover* and *Bloodmania,* both 1970.

Sid shows more range as far as acting in this film. He is almost straight with his hair cut short and an unruffled demeanor. He's the dealmaker here and knows when to get the fuck out of Dodge. The way the film is cut, it looks like he escapers with Linda. But that suit at the end… well, I have nothing to say. Ross Hagen tried for a sequel in 1983, to be called *Warrior Women*. Production was started but the film was never finished. Considering Dr. Tsu and Gregorious survived the first film, it would have been interesting to see a sequel.

WHAT IT MEANS TO BE AN "ICON"
by Joe Ripple

There are many people these days, claiming the title of "Icon." These can range from actors, to sports stars, to singers…anyone who claims some type of performance within their job description.

Then, there are those who are bestowed this honor…mostly by others, because they wouldn't have the ego to do so themselves. These are the people who provide the most to society, whether it be by giving, how they treat people, how they are loved and welcomed by virtue of just being a decent person.

Sid Haig was both.

A staunch supporter of our military members, a dedicated husband and father, a philanthropist and a superstar within the horror community. Sid was as kind as he was generous, giving of his time and friendship to those who sought him out or a few words of his rather blunt counsel. To this point, I'd like to focus on what Sid brought to all of us, in his own boisterous way.

When I was merely working as the head of security for the Horrorfind Weekend Convention, I had the opportunity to interact with Sid on several occasions. His mantra of taking care of the fans that took care of him was unique…never raised his prices, never turned anyone away. Everyone was treated with the kindness that Sid felt each fan deserved. Sid was honored to be a part of any event, flattered to be in any photos, disproportionately available in the bar area for additional time with fans. He became more than an "Icon." He became family.

When I made the leap to hold the very first "Scares That Care!" Charity Weekend, Sid was among the first to ask if he could attend. With any new show that starts up, there are budget issues to take into consideration. I sent Sid an email, explaining that I wasn't sure if there was going to be enough money for a flight and a hotel for him. Sid called me by phone and simply replied "Joe--If you get me a room, I'll buy my own flight. What you are doing is honorable and needed in this world." Because that's what Icons DO. They recognize that there are aspects to this world that are greater than themselves. Greater than any roles they could possibly play. The aspect of helping others, from the heart, with love and happiness.

Over the years, Sid and his wife Suzie made several donations to the "Scares That Care!" charity. Each well over $1,000—and if Sid had a good year, that amount would increase to $2,500 or higher. But he made me promise never to tell anyone what he gave. He didn't want anyone to feel like they were less important, because they were giving less.

I've written this piece for Pete many times. Edited, re-wrote, scrapped the whole thing, started over. Lengthened, shortened, and walked away several times with tears in my eyes. "Scares That Care! Charity Weekend, 2019," was Sid's very last convention. I'm not going to go into the specifics about his looks, because his love and demeanor were still just as present as they were the first day I met him. And I'll never forget what he told me when the show was over.

"Joe, don't ever stop fuckin' doing what you're doing. The world needs it."

I'm not sure if he knew that his time was near. I'm sure that when it was time for him to go into the next realm, that he was worried about his wife, his family, his kids and his fans. He wasn't worried about

himself, or the outcome of his earthly possessions. I'm sure he just wanted to know where his friends were that went before him, and "Where was his table in this big ass room." I think he already knew that there would be those of us who would do our best to keep his memory alive…and help his family.

Sid is gone from us. There will never be another like him. One who put his fans above his profit, his laughter above his tears, and his willingness to help others without sacrificing his morals or his ethics. He is the kind of celebrity that really remembered what it meant to the fans that travelled out to meet him, with huge smile for each, a line as "Captain Spaulding" and a middle finger up in the air.

He simply owned the title of "Icon." And we are all better in this world for knowing Sid Haig.

Until the next time, my friend.

— Joe Ripple Founder and CEO "Scares That Care! Inc."

PIT STOP (1969)
by Doug Waltz

Grant Willard (Brian Donlevy) sponsors new drivers in a new, dangerous form of racing: The figure eight. Pretty simple, the track is a figure eight and you try not to crash as you hurtle through the intersection at top speed. During a street drag race he comes across Rick Bowman (Richard Davalos). He shows him the race and at first Rick thinks it's insane. Especially when he meets local champion, Hawk Sidney (Sid Haig), who wins because he's insane. Never slows down, never brakes at the intersection. All the drivers know it and are afraid for their lives.

Rick is different; he wants to win so he enters the race. And loses. He enters again, and loses again. Finally, third time is the charm and he beats Hawk at the races. He pays for it with a beating from Hawk who destroys Rick's car with an axe and breaks Rick's arm in the process.

This doesn't stop Rick; if anything it makes him hungry to win again and again, not matter what the odds and the cost.

It all leads up to the big race, Hawk and Rick have become friends and decide it's time to pull out all the stops and win a legitimate race for a change. Grant tells Rick that as long as it's one of his cars that wins it doesn't matter what the name of the driver is. Rick takes that as win no matter what.

Pit Stop is an interesting black and white film that immerses you into the racing scene of the time. So many crashed up cars, but we also get a treat when they show us some of the amazing creations of George Barris, the creator of the Adam West Batmobile, amongst many other wild cars.

Jack Hill always delivers a solid film and *Pit Stop* is no different. But, we're here for Sid Haig. As Hawk Sidney you can see that manic intensity that Sid brings to the screen. Wire whip thin and a shock of jet black hair will throw off many Sid Haig fans, but he gives you that immense, maniacal smile and you see him in there. The scene where he single handedly destroys Rick's car with an axe just batters at you, interspersed between the car being smashed and close ups of Sid's face and that wild, insane grin. But it's more than that. Hawk starts out as the king of the roost and when he gets taken down a peg, he reacts like everyone is expecting him to. They think he's insane and, maybe he is…a little. But you can tell towards the end of the film that he has figured out that in the world of racing the cars and the driver's are expendable. It's the moneymen who run the race, no matter who risks their lives, and it softens Hawk around the edges and Sid gives us that to. In a hard-edged movie filled with smoke and grease and crashing and violence, Sid Haig's performance adds another dimension that you write off as a one-note performance.

It's so much more and so subtle you don't realize when he did it.

The ending comes along and you're not ready for this. I actually said, "That's it?" And, of course that's it. Jack Hill knows how to pull you in, wrap your head around what he's doing and then says *seeya* when he's done

A fine film.

Sid as "Hawk Sidney" in Pit Stop. Copyright Jack Hill Productions. All Rights Reserved.

PIT STOP:
JACK HILL AND SID HAIG'S WILD MASTERPIECE
By Aaron AuBuchon

According to pretty much everyone involved with the picture, *Pit Stop* (1969) exists for two reasons: 1.) Director Jack Hill wanted to make an art film; 2) Producer Roger Corman wanted to make a stock car picture.

Chocolate meet peanut butter.

Jack Hill first came to Corman's attention as a talented student at UCLA's famous film school at the dawn of the 1960's. In 1963, Corman had co-produced *Dementia 13*, a film written and directed by then-skyrocketing talent Francis Ford Coppola. When the final film was edited, it came in a bit short in the runtime department, and Coppola was unavailable to shoot additional scenes. So Corman, remembering Hill, hired him to do a couple of days of reshoots. He was very happy with the results.

By the late 1960's stock car racing was huge all over the United States, especially in two regions: Southern California and the Southern United States. At the same time, the drive-in business was booming in the south, thanks to long summers, which allowed them to stay open more days of the year than their northern counterparts, as well as the slow adoption of air conditioning in southern homes, making a relatively cool night outside preferable to one in a hot stuffy house. Corman figured that he could fill drive ins in the south with people who would want to watch a film about a sport that also packed grandstands in the same region. Further, he correctly figured it could be shot pretty easily using actual locations near Hollywood. Again, he remembered Jack Hill who had recently finished his feature film directorial debut with the sexploitation classic *Mondo Keyhole* (1966). Corman, who has based his whole career on making things fast, cheap, and as good as they can be while being fast and cheap, was impressed with the amount of production value Hill had wringed out of his miniscule budget. The legend goes that he went to Hill and said, "I want you to make a stock car film."

"Aww, I want to make an art film next," Hill said.

Corman smiled and said, "Well then, why don't you make an art stock car film?"

What was to follow would be, in my opinion, Hill's most powerfully written and deftly directed film and it would contain the finest performance that Sid Haig would give in his long and storied career.

Originally titled *The Winner,* the oddly titled *Pit Stop* (a racing film that features *zero* pit stops) begins where I wish a lot of films would begin, with a drag race brewing. For over half a century, there have been places in every sizable American town where the folks who care to know such things can find a drag race if they have a hot motored car and a particularly carefree personality. We meet Rick Bowman (Dick Davalos) in a place just like that, casually sauntering onto a preexisting race scene and offering to race for pinks (the ownership of the losing driver's car.) Unknown to

All photos copyright Jack Hill Productions.

Rick, the driver he has chosen to race, his car, and the local race scene itself is bankrolled and controlled by Grant Willard, played by the ever-reliable Brian Donlevy (*The Quatermass Xperiment*) in his final screen role. Willard is an affable pseudo-Svengali-like guy who plays like a stand-in for every overly competitive Greatest Generation father pitting his Baby Boomer "sons" against each other for his affection. The race that ensues, a quick pounder that ends in an accident, attracts the attention of the local constabulary who offer Rick a stay in the hoosegow for the evening.

Willard is no dummy and sees in Rick the exact combination of recklessness and more recklessness that is required for one of his current obsessions, which he introduces to Rick after paying the bail to spring him from the pokey. Figure 8 racing is exactly what it sounds like: stock cars are piloted around a track in the shape of a figure 8, which means that the fastest cars and the slowest cars meet where the 8 connects in the middle, and enormous, bone shattering crashes result. Unlike demolition derby, which happens at relatively low speeds, Figure 8 demands that cars reach literally breakneck speeds, making the eventual crashes especially violent. Racing is inherently dangerous, but Figure 8 racing is just goddamned *insanely* dangerous. In fact, Jack Hill didn't want to make a stock car film at all, but after discovering Figure 8 racing, he felt that it was so nutty, so uniquely American in its bravado (and the stupidity that comes with it), that it and the people who participated in it needed to be documented for posterity. The footage they shot of the racing, the outcome of six weekends spent at the real Ascot Park racetrack in Gardena, California is some of the most bananas racing footage ever committed to celluloid. They took six cameras and shot from six different angles, including right where the cars would meet, often in cataclysmic collisions. Director Hill manned that camera himself, as the production had no insurance and he figured if someone had to man a camera a few feet from where two tons of metal would regularly smash into another two tons of metal at high speed, it should be him.

The crashes are spectacular and edited (by Jack Hill, uncredited) in such a way that they seem to be omnipresent in the event, one after another, constant metal grinding and pounding against metal. Rick Bowman sits, amazed and says, "this is the nuttiest thing I've ever seen." When asked by Willard if he'd like to give it a try, he says he'd rather head back to jail. Hawk Sidney (Sid Haig), the winner of the race, jumps out of his car wide eyed and defiant in the face of an audience who showers him with boos. His subsequent sexual assault on the nearly naked trophy girl is sold as a bit of tomfoolery but earns louder derision from the grandstands. The action shifts over to the bar across from the racetrack, where, Rick, Grant Willard, Hawk and his hanger-on Jolene (Beverly Washburn) get to know each other.

Hawk gives a soliloquy that frames his character and everything about figure 8 racing worth knowing. "Everybody knows you gotta be ding-y to run the figure 8's," he says, heaping unspoken threat on delivered intensity. "You know why I'm the winner? Cause I'm the ding-y-est there is." As the nightclub spins into wild abandon, Rick acknowledges the gauntlet that has been tossed in front of him and decides that he might just be a little bit ding-y himself.

Grant Willard is a businessman, and a shrewd one at that. Though he coaxes Rick onto the track, he apparently requires the drivers to finance their first cars, so Rick makes a deal with local salvage yard owner Luther to use one of the cars from his lot, which Rick will pay for out of the prize money he wins from his first race, which he loses in a pretty spectacular crash. We get an important look at Rick's character after that collision. He climbs out of the car and savagely attacks the other driver; one supposes for having the temerity to crash into him. To reiterate, collisions are a thing that just happen in this form of racing; not too put too fine a point, but it's the *point* of the thing. But Rick takes the collision very personally; violently so. As we get to know him, taking things personally becomes a more important part of his character.

The backup plan to pay Luther for the now-wrecked car is to work at his salvage yard for two bucks an hour until the car is paid off. The gig comes with an added bonus: Rick gets to build himself a new racecar in the evenings. At this point, you have to start asking yourself some questions about Rick Bowman. Here's a guy who appears to be well into his 30s (Dick Davalos was 38 as the film was shot) who suddenly appears in an established race scene with a souped-up gasser but with no money to buy another car when he loses it, and clearly no job to lose when he goes to work in a salvage yard for the 100 hours it would take to repay the $200 bones he promised for the tub he smashed up. Where did this guy come from? Why doesn't he have people, responsibilities, etc.? A lot about Rick Bowman doesn't add up.

While Rick is working one day, Hawk and Jolene show up to get started working on Hawk's new car. He tells Luther and the gang that work for him (I call them The Salvage Yard Layabouts) that he's going to run a big-time race driving a backup car for established racer Ed McCloud (George Washburn). While he's there, Hawk instigates another testosterone-fueled exchange between himself and Rick. There is a playful quality to Hawk's taunting which ends in laughter, a bit of misdirection about what is to come. Hill loved to use the tools at his disposal to lead the audience one direction through plot development, character development, and even the use of clichés and then change direction on them. At this point in the picture, Hawk seems all bluster. He will not remain so.

Rick also has a one-on-one conversation with Jolene during this scene that contains a really important bit of dialogue that you could miss if you're not paying attention. Jolene asks him why he started a fight with the other racer, and he turns the question on her. "I don't know" he shrugs, "It just happens sometimes. I mean, do you always know why you do something?" In asking the question, he's deflecting, trying to make his irrationality seem commonplace. In addition to that bit of thematic content, we get to watch them flirt, setting up the main romantic subplot for Rick.

The next race: Rick and Hawk are at it again. For reasons that make sense only within the logic of the film, the announcer talks nonstop about Rick Bowman, a driver who has previously made one appearance at the racetrack, lost, and was an asshole about it. Much narrated race drama ensues, and we are sure that Rick is going to win this one. He spectacularly doesn't. Again, he crashes, and again he is pissed off when he crashes. As he tries to calm down, he encounters an old man who offers quite a bit of sage advice. Turns out the guy is a former racer (apparently from just after the invention of automobiles) and offers to give Rick some tips which leads to a series of very technical-sounding lessons which bestow a needed edge.

At the next Figure 8 race, Hawk shows up with an impressive California Custom car, and proceeds to threaten all the other drivers with an unspecified but clearly unpleasant outcome should they so much as ding the chrome on the fancy new ride. Understandably, the announcer tells the audience that all eyes are on Hawk's fancy #3 car, and mystifyingly, he further says that many people are also watching the "sensational new driver Rick Bowman" who now sits with a whopping 0-2 record at the track. "I hope someone flips that car tonight" says Rick's buddy (one of The Salvage Yard Layabouts) of Hawk's shiny new car, and so you can guess what happens. Hawk ends up with his fancy car on its lid thanks to some snazzy new racing techniques from Rick Bowman. Hawk is left in the dust, dragging himself out of the upturned vehicle, wheezing and covered with contents of an entire fire extinguisher. Here Hawk's character takes a deadly turn. Up until now, Hawk has been a wide-eyed maniac, laughing and bellowing and generally being a buffoon. The Hawk that emerges is deadly, alarmingly quiet. The same character that hoped Hawk's car would flip over suggests that he seems sore about it. Sid Haig delivers one of his most bone-chilling performances with his answer. If you watch this movie, and don't find yourself wanting to rewind this scene and re-watch Haig deliver acres of visceral threat using nothing more than a low even tone and a flick of the eyes, you and I probably don't have much else to talk about.

Next up: the action is back to the bar across from the track, and I have to admit a certain bias: any film that takes the camera off the tripod, emulating the handheld freedom brought on by exuberant and experimental films being made all over the world in the late 60's, and then points it at sweaty American young people going nuts on a dance floor, you have won all of my attention. If the soundtrack is some kind of burning up-tempo jazz, R&B or straight rock and roll, you have won my heart too. So even if *Pit Stop* didn't have everything else going for it, it would have this astonishingly fun, free dance scene. There are at least a couple of other times that there is similar dancing in the film, but this one is the best. Even rock-solid Rick is out there cutting a rug with Jolene. And when the music slows down, the sweaty energy and the harsh lighting combine to create some astonishingly artful shots. As they leave the bar, Rick and Jolene make plans to shack up for the night, but are first intercepted by a drunk and deranged Hawk

Sidney, who proceeds to beat the shit out of Rick and his gorgeous 58 Ford, menaces Jolene, and lands Rick at the doctor's clinic with a busted arm and a concussion.

Rick makes a beeline to the shop of Ed McCloud, aforementioned racing bigshot, but first encounters his wife Ellen (Ellen Burstyn) and the two spark an awkward sort of chemistry that is broken up when Ed himself shows up and bawls the piss out of Rick for no particularly good reason. At this point, about halfway through the film, we have now met all the really important players and have had their characters set up and the thematic lines drawn. To say much more about plot specifics would be detrimental to the enjoyment of people who are reading this but haven't yet availed themselves of the magic of *Pit Stop*. And I so don't want to do that. I want every person who is interested at this point to watch them film, and preferably the 2017 Arrow version, which looks and sounds amazing.

Why do I find myself returning to this film over and over again? What's so good about it? Well part of it is the sureness of Hill's direction. In talking with Corman, he apparently said "it will be an art film because the hero will lose the big race." Corman, ever practical, said "no Jack, the hero wins the race." Knowing that the film was going to play mostly to an unsophisticated audience famous for needing chicken wire in front of live performers to protect them from thrown bottles and glasses, Corman decided that the film he was paying for couldn't deviate too much from conventional expectation.. So, Hill thought for a while and then said, "okay, he wins the big race, but loses his soul." And that's exactly what happens. *Pit Stop* was a real bit of auteur filmmaking from Hill, who also wrote it, produced it, shot some of it, and edited it. Every frame drips with his intent, and that intention was to subvert audience expectation about character and plot, and deliver a film that was righteously exciting and equally thought provoking.

The look of the film is iconic, which is itself a bit of an irony, as *Pit Stop* was likely less successful than it might have been thanks to its being shot in black and white at a time where black and white was rapidly becoming passé. But according to Sid Haig, the reason for that decision was financial not aesthetic. At the time, color film stocks weren't fast enough to capture the action at a nighttime racetrack, and with a (purportedly) $35,000 budget to get the whole thing done, they couldn't afford the lights they would need to shoot at Ascot Park for the night races. However, the result has a sort of classic feel, and the Arrow restoration adds a deep richness to that greyscale pallet that helps the film feel noir-ish and contributes to its mystique. At the time of its release however, it contributed to a short run and a fast fade to relative obscurity.

The film has a really magical feel for fans of racing and what is now known as kustom kulture. A similar picture done at a studio would have built "race" locations and dressed them to look properly "race-y". *Pit Stop* is a film that didn't have that kind of budget and instead had to rely on real locations where real racers hung out to deliver pre-existing production design, and it delivers so much real feel that it is a treasure to fans of racing who long for the glory days of the mid to late 60's when racing and custom cars were huge all over America and especially in

Southern California. The guy who owned Ascot Park at that time plays the announcer at the track, so they got that role and location for free. The guy who owns the bar that the racers hang out at plays the bartender, so they got that location and actor for free. The guy that plays the doctor in the film is the actual doctor who put the Humpty Dumpty racers back together again when they crashed, and so they got him and the clinic free. Customizing legend George Barris donated his custom shop for shooting in exchange for a cameo in the film. Instead of hiring extras, they asked actual race car drivers, pit crews, track workers and the like to be the background characters. The question became: how do you keep a whole bunch of non-actors, who weren't getting paid to show up and stay the long hours they needed them? According to Haig (in a story he told me a couple of months before he passed away), the way you do it is to call up a local beer distributor and ask them if they'd like to sponsor the film. Because a refrigerator truck packed with beer is a pretty compelling reason to show up and you drinking bucketloads of it because it's free is a pretty compelling reason to remain. At the time it was simple finances that dictated location decisions, but to car aficionados, it's automotive history unfurling in front of their eyes.

Pit Stop is a film that knows what it wants to be, executes its vision deftly, and feels authentic to its audience. If that was all it had going for it, it would be a great film. But it also has some astonishing performances. First, Dick (Richard) Davalos was a method actor, former roommate and friend of James Dean (Davalos shared the screen with him in *East of Eden*, 1955) and a throwback to former age, not long past at the time but accelerating away quickly. Davalos was cast in the same mold as his friend James Dean and Marlon Brando- a quietly emotional even keel that could go off the deep end when poked and prodded. Equally rough and tumble and sensitive, Davalos had a classic American look with an Elvis Presley pompadour and a casual half smile. As the Age of Aquarius was in full swing, an Elvis hero in a race car movie was a real nod to a recent and fairly un-hip past, but Davalos brings a lot of intensity to the character. His delivery of the complicated Rick Bowman is outstanding, compelling, and completely controlled. He knows what he wants that character to be, and it plays. Rick Bowman is strong, driven and wants to be taken very seriously, and as Hill was writing him, he had Dick Davalos in mind for the role.

Sid Haig's Hawk Sidney is almost the opposite of Rick Bowman: wild, wide-eyed, unpredictable. He is equal parts malevolent joke and self-aggrandizement... at least for some of the film. About halfway through the film we see a seriousness that Hawk hadn't displayed up until that point. Was it a new side to his personality? Or maybe it was kept hidden from others? Or, maybe we simply hadn't had a chance to see it yet, as we had only seen Hawk up until that point in a very particular context. But from the shift that comes as a result of his beating of Rick, he grows a depth that broadens the dimensions of what had previously been an entertaining but relatively shallowly plumbed character. We are treated to a post-race exchange between the two men that is probably the most poignant scene in the film. These two rivals decide to become open and vulnerable and completely honest with each other for a moment. All pretense is dropped, and they are themselves, trying to navigate a confusing world where even their own behavior and feelings are mystifying and occasionally alien to them. They come together as two people who recognize in each other a confusion of behavior that is paradoxically known best to those that strive hardest.

And then the character pivots again. You expect that Hawk will now be soft spoken and somewhat morose for the rest of the film also turns out to not be true. He goes back and forth between his old bravado and a brooding seriousness in a way that is really exciting to watch.

As with Dick Davalos, Jack Hill said that he wrote the parts of Hawk and Jolene for Haig and actress Beverly Washburn respectively. And Washburn is extremely good as Jolene, bringing a combination of innocence and sensuality to the role, but the film really belongs to Haig, who according to Jack Hill grew up with people just like the ones in the film during his childhood in Fresno. For his part, Haig felt that Hawk Sidney was "a sort of runaway Dale Earnhardt. More brawn than brains" but that he really liked the switch that Hawk made halfway though. "It was a lot of fun just being crazy. But at the same time it was kind of rewarding to kind of switch into that gentler side," he said during an interview. He went on, "I kind of really liked Hawk Sidney because he was crazy. For some reason I kinda gravitate to these characters that really don't give a shit. They're going *that* way and if you're standing in the way you just might get hurt. In society today, people are more in to getting along than stepping up. So that's part of what I liked about him."

Haig and Hill made a great combo. By the time they did *Pit Stop*, they had already done

three films together, including Hill's senior film *The Host* (1960) at UCLA, and then *Blood Bath* (1966) and *Spider Baby* (1968). He would eventually star in many of Hill's best-known films in the 1970's alongside blaxploitation goddess Pam Grier. He said that Hill gave him very specific ideas about what he wanted in a given scene, and then got out of his way and let him work. The results, especially from *Pit Stop*, show the success of that method.

This is a film that shakes loose the concept of heroes and villains but whose whole plot and thematic structure are built of acts that are both explicitly heroic *and* villainous. And the heroism runs the gamut from traditional tough guy bravery in the face of danger to a more introspective heroism that requires characters to honestly evaluate themselves and their behavior and then decide on their next action. That latter evaluation gives birth to the film's greatest villainy, a soft sort of ugliness that after all isn't the world's greatest sin but is still a form of betrayal to the self that is intended to seem cold and uncaring but instead plays to the other characters and the audience as cowardly and dishonorable. And ultimately, that's what makes this one a masterpiece, I think. We're never sure who these people were before the small bits of their lives that we witness, we have no idea what their real motivations are or what they've been through. Feature film length and convention dictate a certain simplicity of purpose for most character arcs. *Pit Stop* plays on those conventions in such a way that you are sure you know these people until they start behaving not like the usual film characters conveniently wearing white or black hats, but instead behave like real people: mutable and unpredictable as they careen around the track, unsure who they will be when they round the next bend. And in the process, we all get to go for a hell of a wild ride.

SID AND JACK AND PAM
By David Beckham

*Pam Grier, Terry Carter and Jack Hill on-set of **Foxy Brown**.*
Photographer unknown. All Rights Reserved.

"Sid Haig and Pam Grier were my Tracy and Hepburn." Jack Hill gave both Pam and Sid there break in movies. While Pam is credited as an extra in *Beyond the Valley of the Dolls* it was her first film with Jack *The Big Doll House* that brought her to Grindhouse attention. For the follow up, *The Big Bird Cage*, it was Pam and Sid that worked up the opening song and dance.

But before there was Pam and Sid, there was Sid himself. When Jack was still in film school, his student film was *The Host*, inspired by Jack's reading of *The Golden Bough*. Jack had the backing of Dorothy Arzner, of the Pasadena Playhouse, and when he was looking for someone to play the lead, Dorothy recommended Sid. Jack credits Dorothy not for only being a great teacher of young filmmakers and actors, but also a great sponsor, putting together life-long collaborations. Sid became his favorite actor. *The Host* is one of the few films Jack made that you can't easily find on a streaming service. It has appeared on DVD as an extra on *Switchblade Sisters* and the Arrow Blu-Ray of *Spider Baby*. In addition to *The Host*, Jack and Sid made seven features together, and Jack wrote each role especially for Sid, but even then, it was still a collaboration. Sid always brought more to the part than what was on the page.

The timeline of the films run into and over each other. *Blood Bath / Track of the Vampire* (Arrow Video) was the first feature for Jack (outside of uncredited additions to *The Wasp Woman*, *The Terror*, and *Dementia 13*). Sid plays a bohemian artist in the comic interludes between the horror scenes, along with Carl Schanzer, who co-starred in *Spider Baby* and Jonathan Haze of *Little Shop of Horrors* fame. Blood Bath was originally a Yugoslavian Film called "Operation Titan" and Jack was hired by Roger Corman to turn it into something that grindhouse audiences would watch. Jack brought in Sid, John and Carl to shoot the filler scenes, and got William Campbell (*Hush, Hush, Sweet Charlotte* and the *Star Trek* episode, *The Trouble With Tribbles*) who had starred in *Titan* to shoot additional scenes that would turn the former spy movie into a psycho thriller.

Working with Sid was the highlight of *Blood Bath*, which Jack completed in 1964. The movie wasn't finished, as far as Roger Corman was concerned though. Jack says Roger brought in "Whats-her-Name" to expand the movie to a longer running time, and she turned the once spy thriller / then psycho killer movie / into a bloodless vampire flick that doesn't really make any sense.

In *Spider Baby* Sid stars as Ralph, an adult-child regressing to infant-hood. Like every Jack Hill collaboration, the part could only have been played by Sid. Shaving his head for the first time, Sid also shaved off his beard and mustache to look like a giant, gawky baby. His first appearance, curled up on the floorboard of Lon Chaney Jrs. motor car, drooling like an idiot, then sparking to life as he recognizes his little sisters, is unforgettable. Sid was willing to do anything the part required. He wore the Little Lord Fauntelroy outfit, a couple of sizes too small, without complaint. He hung upside-down outside Carol Ohmart's window watching her undress (who wouldn't) until he almost passed out. And every moment Sid is on screen, even with the twenty something Beverly Washburn and the under-age Jill Banner, you cannot take your eyes off him. He is a joyful lunatic.

After *Spider Baby*, Jack and Sid re-teamed for *Pit Stop* (aka *The Winner*) for Roger Corman. This time Corman let Jack have complete control, as long as he made a movie about Stock Car Racing and brought it in on budget. Jack has always been able to bring a picture in on cost, and he can make any subject interesting, especially with Sid along. Corman's name doesn't even appear as producer on this one, it's all Jack and Sid. *Pit Stop* takes the rags-to-riches to Redemption story-line and lets the hero fall. It is Sid, who looks to be the films bad-guy as the movie begins, that becomes, if not it's hero, at least it's soul.

Sid plays "Hawk Sidney" (a convolution of Sid Haig) the guy everyone wants to beat. The guy who should be the hero (Richard Davalos, *East of Eden*) finally does, but it's when he tries to steal Hawk's girlfriend that Sid takes it personal. He beats the Holy Shit out of him and his car. After losing a second race, Hawk has to admit that his rival "rode a hell of a race," and offers to buy him a beer. It's not a set-up for another trouncing. It's real. *Pit Stop* is probably not the Jack Hill / Sid Haig movie you think of first, but for Jack, he considers it to be his most personal, and maybe even the best. It's available as a Special Edition 2 disc Blu Ray from Arrow Video, as well as a single disc from Scorpion Releasing.

Now getting back to Sid and Pam. It didn't matter how much screen time they shared, just the energy they brought to a movie made it rise above bigger budgeted films. Jack, Sid and Pam made two Philippine Jungle Women's Prison flicks and two of the best Blaxploitation movies ever.

1971 brought *The Big Doll House*, with Grier as "Grear" the dominant (but not butch) lesbian prisoner. As part of Pam's plan to break out of prison, she lets Sid (as a sleazy delivery man) play with her tits, and then moves his hand down to her goody box. Sid doesn't get away that easy though. Another female inmate pins him against a wall, puts a knife to his groin and demands, "Get it up, or I'll cut it off!" With Viagra still nearly 3 decades away, Sid has no choice but to work it on his own. Jack says of the female on male rape, "I wasn't trying to be subversive, I just thought it was funny."

Sid and Pam made a couple of other pictures together in the Philippines, including *Black*

Mama White Mama, but it was *The Big Bird Cage* where they really had some fun. Jack cast Sid as the Revolutionary Leader "Django" and Pam as his sometimes willing second in command "Blossom." Sid plays it all for laughs which is why his work with Jack shines. Jack's sense of humor was perfect for the 70's. It doesn't matter what a person is, color, race, sex-preference... if it's funny, do it. So a self-serving hippy with less interest in "The Revolution" and more interest in tonight's feast was a perfect role for Sid. It didn't matter how goofy it was, Sid did it. Sid is also credited as 2nd Unit Director on *The Big Bird Cage*, but Jack doesn't remember anything about that. He says that was either a mistake, or Corman padding out the credits. *The Big Doll House* and *The Big Bird Cage* are available along with *Women in Cages* from Shout Factory.

Back in Los Angeles, things weren't so funny. Jack, Pam and Sid were still a team, but it was Pam's world now. *Coffy* was the first, and probably the best, of the Lady-Vigilante Blaxploitation movies. Unlike the Women's Prison films, *Coffy* is short on laughs, but much bigger on violence. Exploding heads before *Scanners*. Lynchings. Rape. Forced drug addiction. And Sid as a particularly mean bastard named Omar. In *The Big Bird Cage* and *The Big Doll House* it really didn't matter if a character was played by a white, black or Asian actor (for the most part). Sid and Pam were lovers and race didn't matter. This time Sid was a racist, cruel, and it was a stretch to play. Jack had faith that Sid could do this, but Sid didn't like being this kind of a bad guy. Sid had often been cast as the bad guy in other productions, but this one got him typecast as mean. *Coffy* is OOP on Blu-Ray from Olive Films and still available on DVD from MGM/UA.

The final film of our trio was *Foxy Brown*, and it too was a more violent, less humorous, but still very popular hit. Jack didn't want to write another heavy role for Sid, so instead cast him in a smaller role as an airplane pilot. There just wasn't a lot in the story for Sid to do, but I wanted him to be in the movie, so I wrote him this part. By the time Jack was ready to make his next movie, *The Swinging Cheerleaders,* Sid's agent was asking more than the producer's budget would allow. *Foxy Brown* is still available on Blu-Ray from Olive Films.

Jump ahead to 1982 and Jack Hill's final film, *Sorceress*. Jack doesn't have a lot of good things to say about *Sorceress*. This is the film that made him want to leave filmmaking behind.

He wrote a part, specifically for Sid, and Sid was willing, but Roger Corman was not going to shell out the cash. The budget kept getting cut, smaller and smaller, and the final film does not have a directed by Jack Hill credit. The movie made money, but Jack was frustrated with it all, and wanted out.

Sid wanted out too. By 1990 he was tired of always playing the heavy and he stopped working in film. But then home video was really taking hold and Jack was back. He wasn't making new movies, but his films were being seen again, by people like Rob Zombie and Quentin Tarantino. And Sid came back too. When Rolling Thunder released Jack's *Switchblade Sisters* they put up the funds to finish post-production on *The Host*. When Dark Sky released *Spider Baby*, Sid did the commentary with Jack. Now there is talk of a Jack Hill Box set from Arrow Video, similar to the Herschell Gordon Lewis box set a few years back. All is pending U.S. rights issues.

But there will never be another collaboration between Jack and Sid. Jack kindly agreed to the interview about his relationship with Sid. He has fully retired from filmmaking He is happy.

Jack's father, Roland E. Hill was a pilot at the end of World War I. He also was a motion picture Art Director (including on several of Jack's films) and he designed Sleeping Beauty's Castle at Disneyland. Jack has published a collection of his father's letters. I highly recommend that you read them. They are available for Kindle.

Jack at the editing bay. Photographer unknown. All rights reserved.

WOMAN HUNT: SID AT HIS SLEAZY BEST

It was 1972 and I was drive in bound one evening with cooler full of beer, some weed and bad intentions. The Morris Plains Drive In was showing a film with the catchy title Woman Hunt, so I decided to check it out. Drunk and stoned, I have scattered memories of this film, but being that it is a Sid film, I needed to revisit it. Problem was it isn't out in any format. Thanks go to Doug Waltz, who found me a copy from somewhere to include here.

Another low-budget take on *The Most Dangerous Game*, produced by John Ashley and Eddie Romero, Romero also directed. and written by Jack Hill.

John Ashley stars with Pat Woodell, with Sid Haig third billed as Silas, a sleazy boat captain all employed by Spyros, a crazy rich man living in an island fortress. Spyros is played by Eddie Garcia (Dr. Lorca from *Beast of Blood*). Tony, Silas, and Karp (Ken Metcalfe) kidnap women for Spyros to hunt down. Spyros is a monster who rapes his victims and has a leather clad lesbian to help him.

Five women are trapped on Silas's boat as he holds them at gunpoint. Tony (Ashley) is not down with any of this. Spyros summons him and tells Tony that he no longer has use for him. Tony finds a half drunk Silas waiting for him with a gun. Silas tells Tony that Spyros ordered him to "Take Tony out when it's convenient." Silas drunkenly chuckles that, "Right now isn't convenient." Tony decides to grab the girls and escape.

Silas has the hots for the black girl that was captured. He smacks her around before reaching the fortress and Karp tells him that they will settle this soon. Silas baits him , laughing. Sid plays Silas as a redneck. One girl, Magda, gets a visit from Karp who tells her that he can help her get out. He gets her naked, then spits on her, calling her a pig that going to slaughter. This breaks her will.

Spyros has a group of five fellow rich bastards visit him. He wines and dines them, then promises them a night with the girls before they hunt them down. When one of them curse Spyros out and goes to leave, Spyros shoots him with a cross bow. One of Spyros's abused captives gets a gun and escapes. Spyros orders Silas to get the girls back to their rooms. Billie, Charlene Jones) the black girl, seduces Silas. She flashes her tits at him and the drunken Silas falls down trying to get his shirt off. Then he passes out in her bed.

Tony finds Spyros's lesbian henchwoman trying to munch the carpet of McGee (Pat Woodell). They tie her up and find Billie with the passed out Silas. They free the other girls and go looking for weapons. Tony kill the power and they kill a couple of guards as they arm themselves. Spyros has tracked down the escaped girl and ,while the others watch in horror, he rapes and kills her in front of them. One guy wants out , so Karp goes after him and cuts his throat.

Guards shoot one of the escaping women, then they are mowed down in a hail of bullets by Tony. Karp find Silas just waking up and they have words. After Silas flips Karp off, Karp kills him. Magna falls and breaks a leg. She says she can't go on. She asks for a weapon and seeks cover. Spyros and his group walk into her ambush. Now things get bloody. One of the rich hunter's head explodes in a shower of gore. She machine guns Karp, but Spyros cuts her down.

Copyright New World Pictures. All Rights Reserved.

To complicate matters, Billie gets bitten by a cobra. Tony kills it, but Billie dies. The next morning Spyros find that while they slept, the rich guys and Spyros's men took off. It's just Spyros and his henchwoman. Tony makes one of those "pull a branch back and put spikes on it" traps. The woman walks right into it. Spyros puts her out of her misery with a bullet to the head.

Tony and McGee get naked and are screwing in a creek. Spyros, bloodily wounded, is about to machine gun them. He has second thoughts before his head explodes and he plunges into the water. Now did someone shoot him or did he do himself in? We never know because it ends with Tony and McGee finding a village.

Another one of those weird, downbeat '70s endings. The film is pretty bloody, almost harkening back to the *Blood Island* films. For whatever reason Ashley is pretty subdued here, looking very distracted. Pat Woodell was no stranger to these films having appeared in *The Big Doll House* and *The Twilight People*. Sid is great as Silas and chews a lot of scenery. Things perk up when he is on camera and his character is a slimy bastard who fucks up and pays the price.

Oddly this film just vanished after its release. Sid said in an interview that maybe three people might have seen it. Read the interview in this issue about Sid and his cut scene with a water buffalo. This film begs for a DVD or Blu Ray treatment.

CREATURE COMFORT:
My Oblivious Contribution To Box Office History
by Ross Snyder

In the Fall of 2011, while watching a late-night wrestling show, I caught an interesting advertisement during one of the commercial breaks. A new horror film entitled *Creature* was apparently opening nationwide in theaters on Friday. This development was intriguing to me for a couple of reasons. First off, I had never heard a peep about this film before. As an avid movie goer and enthusiast, I find that most genre features that are opening on a nationwide platform are usually at least on my radar before their advertisements starts hitting the network channels. Despite all that, *Creature* was apparently barreling into multiplexes with little to no fanfare, all while carrying the foreboding admonishment that "Terror Has Teeth"!

Secondly, Creature was toting top billing from legendary, exploitation actor Sid Haig. By 2011, Sid was experiencing a flourishing career resurgence following his portrayal of the Captain Spaulding character in the films of Rob Zombie. While not a fan of Zombie's output myself, I, like most cult film aficionado worth their salt, always relished the on screen appearance of Sid dating back to his frequent collaborations with exploitation auteurs like Jack Hill, Eddie Romero, and Fred Olen Ray in the '70s and '80s. Sid's new found notoriety garnered him a whole new generation of fans and made him a popular draw at horror conventions around the globe. It also led to his appearance in a glut of low budget genre fare, the kind that would have undoubted littered the shelves of video stores nationwide, had the majority not shuttered their doors nearly ten years prior.

Lastly, *Creature* surprisingly appeared to be a good old fashioned, southern fried, man in a suit, swamp monster movie in the tradition of *Terror In The Swamp*, Don Barton's *Zaat*, and Larry Buchanan's *Curse Of The Swamp Creature*. To get a little perspective on the state of the horror genre at the time, 2011's two top grossing horror films were *Paranormal Activity*

3 and *Insidious*, a sobering reminder that the found footage and creepy ghost child tropes of the '90s were still in full swing nearly 15 years later (and are sadly still a viable box office draw today). The rubber suit creature feature was a primarily forgotten commodity in the post-CGI, cinematic landscape so the sudden appearance of one was certainly an eyebrow raiser for me. Although my curiosity was peaked, my initial assumption was that a drive-in style, hillbilly monster romp in the year 2011 would probably not be a box office boffo. But more on that later.

*Sid as "Chopper" in **Creature**. Copyright The Bubble Factory. All Rights Reserved.*

Lo and behold, after some quick research, it appeared that *Creature* was indeed coming to one loan multiplex near me in Parsippany, NJ. I secured myself tickets for a Saturday matinee screening and took along my mother and grandmother. My mom is a lifelong horror fiction and film lover and my grandma (who was in her nineties at the time but still very active) had a penchant for the "dumb kids getting killed in the woods" sub-genre, so I figured that Creature may just score as a home run for an afternoon family outing. Not surprising, upon entering the theater we found ourselves completely alone aside from one loan couple, who I'm guessing either wandered in by accident or perhaps were unsuspectingly subjected to the Creature promo on cable like myself.

After a prologue featuring a fully nude, skinny dipping female having her legs bitten off by an unseen entity, Creature kicks off with the customary introduction to its central carload of teenage gator bait, who are traversing through the Cajun backwoods en route to New Orleans. The gang (who seem like they would never be friends in real life) is comprised of three couples; two ex-military muscle heads, their girlfriends, and a comedy relief brother and sister team. Sid pops up as Chopper, the proprietor of a roadside tourist trap offering weary travelers gas, cold beers, and an outhouse around back. It's here at Chopper's that the seemingly oblivious gang learns about the legend of Lockjaw, a half man / half alligator mutant that stalks the local swamplands. This southern fried version of Bigfoot was supposedly responsible for countless murders and disappearances throughout the bayou, which eventually led to the closing of the once thriving Fort Collins mine. And just in case that urban legend isn't enough to crack your crawdads, Lockjaw also has a brain damaged, Kafka-esque origin story that's certain to gussy up your gumbo. Seems several years back in an isolated cabin nearby, an inbred man named Grimly impregnated his last remaining sister / wife in an attempt to preserve his family's bloodline. Sadly, she was snapped up and devoured by a giant white alligator named Anon right before Grimly's eyes.

In pursuit of vengeance, Grimly tracked Anon to his lair and killed the beast with his bare hands before tearing him into pieces and eating every ounce of the gator raw like a steaming bowl of etouffee. This inexplicably caused Grimly to mutate into Lockjaw and roam the gator infested countryside in search of a new human bride to procreate with. The kicker here is that the comic relief brother and sister team turn out to be Chopper's son and daughter, a voyeuristic and incestual redneck duo who have apparently been posing as "city folks" in a cunning ruse to lure their new friends to the bayou as potential mates (or supper) for Lockjaw. Seems the locals apparently worship Lockjaw as a sort of deity and regularly offer up female sacrifices for his breeding pleasure. Once things start to go sour, even Sid gets in on the act by tying his daughter to a chair, chopping off her foot with a machete, and leaving her on display as a possible plaything for the horny gator man. With an endearing monster suit, dollops of sleaze and gore (which instigated MPAA censorship), and quite possibly the most random and impromptu lesbian hookup scene in cinema history, *Creature* is the kind of raucous and mindless fun that overflowed the drive-in screens of yesteryears. That being said, its African American lead surviving until the end and defeating the monster (with the help of a very convenient sinkhole) is probably Creature's most subversive cinematic act.

Without giving Creature much of a second thought following my initial viewing, I woke up to some very interesting news on Monday morning. A gaggle of entertainment news agency including ABC, The Telegraph, and The Guardian were all reporting a similar story; *Creature* was apparently the worst performing film in box office history. *Creature* was screened in wide release on over 1,500 screens throughout the U.S. and grossed a paltry $331,000 on its opening weekend. To break it down, that means that each of its screenings throughout the weekend were attended by fewer than 6 people. It grossed approximately $220 per theater which is less than what one row of theater goers typically spend on popcorn at an average multiplex screening. Surprisingly, this disastrous distribution schematic was the brainchild of a different Sid, legendary producer Sid Sheinberg. Sheinberg was the former president of Universal / MCA Pictures and is generally credited for discovering Steven Spielberg. Under Sheinberg's leadership, Universal produced and released *Jaws, E.T.,* and *Jurassic Park*, which were the highest-grossing films of the last three decades of the twentieth century.

After MCA was sold to Seagrams in 1995, Sheinberg started the production company The Bubble Factory (along with his two sons) with the intention of producing films independently for potential distribution by Universal. Unfortunately, after the disappointing box office performance of their preliminary productions such as *Flipper* (1996) and *McHale's Navy* (1997), Universal cut ties and The Bubble Factory became a solely independent operation. In 2011, Sheinberg saw fit to greenlight *Creature* (which was produced and directed by the husband and wife team of Fred and Kerry Andrews) with no major studio backing. His plan was to essentially self-distribute it with the intent of creating a new template for indie films to be released on a national platform. For promotion, he purchased low-cost spots on NBCU cable channels and attempted a viral social media campaign, a marketing avenue that was clearly alien to a media dinosaur like Sheinberg. For better or for worse, the results spoke for themselves.

Oddly, I look back fondly on my theatrical experience of viewing *Creature* in a nearly empty multiplex and contributing about $30 of my hard earned smackeroos to one of the lowest grossest film in cinema history. I recently discovered an archival interview with director Fred Andrews from the time of *Creature*'s release in which he claims he would send a signed theatrical poster to anyone who could send him photographic proof of a purchased theater ticket. Had I known of this development at the time, I would have most certainly taken Fred up on his offer.

Grindhouse Purgatory: Sid Haig Memorial Issue

GP writer Ken Brunette with Sid.

*With David Arquette in **Bone Tomahawk**. (Copyright Caliber Media Company.)*